Accelerated Learning
A User's Guide

Alistair Smith ◈ Mark Lovatt ◈ Derek Wise

Crown House Publishing Company LLC
www.CHPUS.com

Accelerated Learning: A User's Guide

Grade Level: 1–12

© 2005 by Alistair Smith, Mark Lovatt, and Derek Wise

Printed in the United States of America

ISBN: 1904424724

Published by:
Crown House Publishing Company LLC
4 Berkeley Street
Norwalk, CT 06850
www.CHPUS.com
Tel: 866-272-8497
Fax: 203-852-9619
E-mail: info@CHPUS.com

This edition is adapted from a book originally published 2003 in the U.K. by Network Educational Press Ltd., P.O. Box 635, Stafford, ST16 1BF.

U.S. editing: Kirsteen Anderson
Design, typesetting, and cover: Dan Miedaner

Library of Congress Cataloging-in-Publication Data

Smith, Alistair, 1957-
 Accelerated learning : a user's guide / Alistair Smith, Mark Lovatt, and
Derek Wise.
    p. cm.
 Includes bibliographical references and index.
 ISBN 1-904424-72-4 (alk. paper)
 1. Educational acceleration. I. Lovatt, Mark. II. Wise, Derek. III.
Title.
 LB1029.A22S65 2005
 370.15'23–dc22
                          2004028819

Contents

Contents

Preface

Accelerated Learning: A User's Guide pulls together new and innovative thinking about learning, offering contemporary solutions to old problems. It is based on the Accelerated Learning model, which, in turn, is underwritten by an informed theoretical understanding.

The term *Accelerated Learning* can be misleading. The method is not for a specific group of learners, nor for a given age range, nor for a category of perceived ability. The method is not about doing the same things faster. It is not about fast-tracking or about accelerating growth. It is a considered, generic approach to learning based on research drawn from disparate disciplines and tested with different age groups and different ability levels in very different circumstances. As such, it can be adapted and applied to very different challenges. *Accelerated Learning* builds from the Accelerated Learning Cycle, of which we provide a simplified and updated version.

Banzai versus Kamikaze

In the Algarve region of Portugal there is a theme park called Aqualand. It is very popular with tourists and has as many as two thousand visitors daily in the height of the summer season. Aqualand is, as its name implies, a water-based theme park. There are rides of varying degrees of challenge, ranging from the leisurely and middle-aged Waterfall to the near-suicidal and testosterone-fueled Kamikaze. Participants in every ride are good humored despite lengthy lines. Watching the visitors making their choices, waiting in line, and eventually taking part in the different rides is fascinating.

Kamikaze is perhaps the most popular ride, followed by Banzai. Waterfall is strictly for the old, the lethargic, and the sane. Kamikaze involves a seventy-five-foot drop into a pool. The drop is close to vertical and you sit on a big aluminum sled to do it. Banzai is higher and longer but has no sled. You lie on your back and hope for the best. The refusal rate for Kamikaze is high. There are virtually no refusers for Banzai. Given that long lines are involved for each, the vast majority of riders are adolescents, and both rides are very high, it is interesting that one ride instills more fear than the other.

With Kamikaze you drop into a long pool surrounded on three sides by those waiting to get their turn with the sled. Everyone is looking at you. You climb a long spiral staircase after you have received a sled. Because the number of sleds is limited, the numbers on the stairway are limited. As you get to the top, you feel the wind blowing and you look out over the whole of the park. You are on your own and everyone is watching. It takes time to get into position. You place your sled on a flat table and get on the sled. There are handles on the front for you to hold on to. You and the sled then sit there until the table slowly tips up. You are held in place by a retractable board. When you are ready you say so, and the operator flips the switch to drop the board. When the board drops, so do you and, veins bulging, you plummet downward. It is at this tipping point that there are the most refusers. Not surprising perhaps? You have yet to commit; you have spent a long, slow, and lonely time getting to this point; and you are asked to sit facing down seventy-five feet of steel shaft as your body gradually tips. What makes committing difficult is that your friends are no longer able to help you, there is no one else doing it alongside you, and you can see the drop in its entirety. Your willingness to say "go" has become a test.

Now consider Banzai. It is higher than Kamikaze and the pool you plummet into is smaller and narrower. Few people other than your friends watch. You drop for longer, from a higher point, and at times, on a similar trajectory. The line is up a wide stairway, however. Groups of youngsters go together and cajole each other as they go. There is social interaction all the way up. The wind still blows, the view spreads out in front and below you, but the experience is an altogether cheerier one for being shared. As you get to the top, you look down on Kamikaze below. There are others lining up beside you to take their turn. Then, at the appropriate moment, you lie down on your own open plastic channel and wait. Eventually, the attendant gives a desultory wave and you launch yourself down feet-first. No sleds or retractable boards are needed. Some seconds later you realize that you are traveling far too fast to sit up and look around, indeed far too fast to do anything except wobble uncontrollably. You splash into the pool at the bottom fifteen seconds later wearing what remains of your swimsuit. You then giggle uncontrollably between mouthfuls of chlorinated water as you fight off the shock.

Accelerated Learning contains many references to spiral staircases, cycles of learning, challenging environments, anxiety and performance, personal commitment, and memorable experiences! We take the view that Banzai learning is generally better for all-around performance than Kamikaze learning. This does not mean there is not a place for personal challenge, but an excessive focus on passing the test can lead to isolation. So too does a lonely and unsupported climb toward that test. Challenge is important for our model of learning. After all, good learning occurs in environments characterized by high challenge and low anxiety. Good learning also involves risk, but not necessarily the winner-takes-all risk of public exposure.

Good learning is not about taking the fastest and most expedient route. Terrifying experiences may be memorable, but often for the wrong reasons. Many refuse the Kamikaze challenge. This is partly because of social isolation—being placed in an unnatural physical situation with skeptical onlookers monitoring your every move. We believe that learning is in part a social construction: People learn from, through, and around others. Providing support along the way is part of the learning model.

Many have found the Accelerated Learning approach valuable. It has played a significant part in provoking thought about the nature of learning and teaching and what should and should not underpin classroom-based approaches to teaching. It is, of course, a model and, like all other models, means different things to each end user. We have deliberately laid bare our thinking behind the model so that you can test the theory and develop your own by-products. *Accelerated Learning* is a valuable tool to take with you on a challenging journey. It is not a sled on an express and very fast route to success but more of a gentle, friendly, and reassuring push to help you on your way.

Alistair Smith
August 2003

Acknowledgments

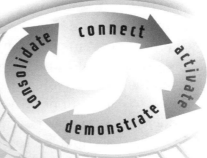

Special thanks to Ani and all the team at Alite for an exciting journey.

.... *Alistair Smith*

Thanks to my family: Jane for everything, and Hannah and Jacob for being such spectacular kids.

Thanks also to friends and colleagues in the teaching profession who are "walkin' the talk" on a daily basis. I hope you find this useful.

.... *Mark Lovatt*

To all the staff and students of Cramlington Community High School. Your talents, creativity, open-mindedness, and willingness to try out new ideas have made this book possible.

.... *Derek Wise*

Accelerated Learning: The Principles

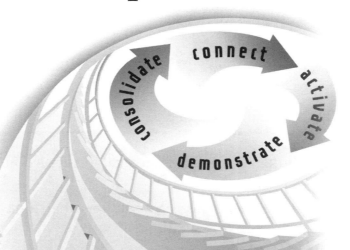

In Chapter 1 You Will Find

- ▶ How to Use This Book
- ▶ Learning Principles Underpinning This Book
- ▶ Why You Should Use Accelerated Learning
- ▶ Creating the Learning Environment
- ▶ Questions to Ask Yourself
- ▶ What Do Your Students Think? Student Questionnaire
- ▶ Motivating Learners
- ▶ Principles of Accelerated Learning
- ▶ What the Principles of Accelerated Learning Mean

How to Use This Book

A good book is a lifetime of experience.

This book provides an easily accessible summary of what Accelerated Learning methods can offer. It is organized into four chapters. Chapter 1 gives the background to the Accelerated Learning approach. Chapter 2 describes the use of the Accelerated Learning Cycle. Chapter 3 gives some advice on enhancing memory. Chapter 4 summarizes good ideas to improve learning. The appendix provides some useful resources.

There are a number of possible ways of making this, or any book, work for you.

You could

- flip through the entire book quickly, taking in section headings as you go, then read.

- scratch and sniff! Dip into the sections that look most useful or interesting.

- begin with the contents page—this gives an overview, or big picture, in advance and primes your learning.

- complete the questionnaire on pages 104–105.

- ask your students to complete the student questionnaire on page 10.

- begin at the beginning, and plow through until the end.

- try out some of the activities that accompany each section and see for yourself how your students respond.

- start with the question-and-answer section on pages 87–90.

- start with the key word list provided in the index and do a key word search throughout the book.

- try to summarize the text for someone else.

- lend the book to someone and get him or her to summarize it for you.

- put it under your pillow and sleep on it.

We have brought together a lot of practical experience in this book, and the challenge has been to pare it down to the bare minimum. We hope you enjoy our minimalism.

Learning Principles Underpinning This Book

I know where I'm going; I know who's going with me.

- All meaningful learning involves risk; good teachers help learners negotiate risk.
- Anxiety paralyzes performance; good teachers provide structured challenge.
- Learning is about seeking and securing connections; good teachers take lots of opportunities to make connections.
- Learning is best done through active engagement; good teachers offer choice, provide a balance of multisensory approaches, and plan for differences among learners.
- Learning accelerates when learners generate multiple meanings (that is, interpret the essential information in their own way and are given safe opportunities to express this interpretation through debate, visuals, dramatizations, case studies, and so on); good teachers provide structured opportunities for learners to reflect, ask questions, hypothesize, and do so through meaningful language exchange.
- Learning needs spaced rehearsal and reflection for consolidation (remembering new information) and transfer (using new information beyond the classroom and school settings); good teachers leave space for this to occur.
- We recommend a cycle for engaging learners that has at least four stages, as shown in the figure.

Four Stage Accelerated Learning Cycle

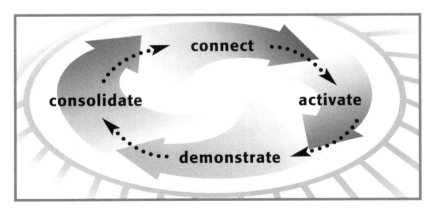

- Good teachers use a coherent model of learning.
- Motivation is shaped by complex variables driven by curiosity; good teachers understand the need for a variety of motivational strategies.
- The best teaching is distinctive and engaging; good teachers make learning memorable.

Why You Should Use Accelerated Learning

A wise man proportions his belief to the evidence.

Are you the same person you were when you first attended school all those years ago? Look out some old photographs and ask yourself that question. We would argue that this generation of schoolchildren brings a significantly different set of qualities and experiences to their learning than did previous generations, and this alone means we should constantly rethink what we teach and how.

1. Families have changed.

Thirty years ago, 85 percent of children were living in a two-parent family unit. Today in the United States the figure is nearer 70 percent, and only 64 percent of those children are living with both biological parents. The concept of family has changed. More combinations of units are recognized and accepted. Roles within families have also shifted. Changing patterns of employment, including more shift work, part-time work, and portfolio working (assembling several sources of employment to make up the equivalent of full-time work), has meant the end of a job for life and the conventional notion of a single breadwinner. The concept of community has shifted too. Schools need to accommodate such shifts in their thinking.

2. Leisure is more individualized.

More leisure activities now take place in two sites—neither of which is outside in the neighborhood, where children used to play. One is the home and the second is shared leisure space—such as recreation centers, multiplexes, or malls. We now adapt our leisure activities to suit individual rather than group preferences. Much of our leisure now involves vicarious participation. Most homes have a personal computer. We can watch sports on large flat screens, from the comfort of the sofa.

3. There are more survivors in our classrooms.

More children are being born prematurely, and more of those are surviving birth. The rate of premature birth increased 29 percent between 1981 and 2002, and a startling percentage of those babies are surviving. Of babies born at 24 weeks, 40 percent survive, and for babies born after 28 weeks that percentage rises to 90 percent. This success comes with attendant problems of low birth weight, including learning difficulties, higher susceptibility to illness, and long-term health problems. The advances in vaccination programs also contribute to more children surviving, and more of them are in our schools.

4. We are not as healthy.

Children are bombarded with messages about convenience foods. Serious scientific debate is considering whether junk food is addictive. Obesity among children in the United States has never been so high. Some 15 percent of children and adolescents are obese (that is, more than 10 percent over their ideal weight). Doctors suggest that the subsequent health problems will eventually be more costly to the nation than smoking- or alcohol-related illness. Research shows again and again the link between improved academic performance and regular exercise.

5. We teach information migrants.

The contemporary fourteen-year-old can multitask beyond the dreams of previous generations. Your sons or daughters can be participating on three floors of an Internet chat room with three different personalities; listening to music they have selected, collated, and downloaded; text messaging their friends; and doing their homework at the same time! Using the prevailing technology of the age, children become foragers, surfers, novelty seekers, and information migrants.

6. We have become time-shifters.

The time lines within which we live our lives differ from those of previous generations. We are increasingly being encouraged to live 24/7 lives. In the United States, cereal manufacturers are discovering that boxed cereal sales are dropping because many adults do not find the time to eat at home. In response, manufacturers are developing finger-friendly products that can be eaten on the run. In the home the refrigerator has become the social center. Individuals in the home operate on different time regimes, but most schools shut their doors between four and five o'clock.

7. Certainties are fewer.

Life has fewer certainties. The age of leaving school and finding a job for life is gone. Frequent career changes or combinations of part-time jobs loom for a section of the workforce. For the rest, service and tourist industry work, job losses to outsourcing, and difficulty obtaining health insurance and other benefits loom. Despite this, we are actively encouraged to create our own "designs for life" and create our own scripts. We buy into stories that support our chosen life script and the agencies in our lives pander to those stories. Reality television sells the dream that anyone can be a pop star. Research suggests that successful and happy young learners are more likely to place value in family and friends than in unrealistic life scripts.

8. Where are the role models?

Many children no longer form a social group with those who live in homes nearby. Some stranger danger programs teach children to be afraid of all unfamiliar adults. Which groups do they relate to and identify with? Where are the role models for maturing youngsters? Role models abound but often they promote uncertainty rather than remove it. Pop stars flirt with androgyny, sports stars look angelic but have their aggression analyzed in fine detail, politicians have their personal lives turned into soap operas.

9. Technology is pervasive and penetrating.

In our childhoods it was said that hover technology would change our lives forever. It never did. This was in part because it never became pervasive. In contrast, information technologies are changing lives in a way that is unprecedented. Statistics about Internet hits, text messages sent, or hours spent watching any of the world's half-million television channels make compelling reading because of what they say about the penetration of technology into our lives. Sources of information abound, but in the midst of this there remains a powerful need for a guide to help us navigate safely through this information. This is why educators will never become redundant. Educators teach the skills of scrutiny, the ability to discern propaganda and bias, and the capability of using the information tools in a life shaped by moral and value-driven considerations.

10. It's different out there!

The spirit of the age differs from that of thirty or forty years ago. This generation of children experiences more autonomy, more choice, and more freedoms with fewer responsibilities and yet have more tests and examinations, more physical constraints, and more anxiety in their lives. Do today's children physically mature earlier? Some evidence supports the view that puberty begins earlier for this generation of schoolchildren. This is the generation with Ritalin at one end and Prozac at the other—a generation being "taught" emotional intelligence in schools.

> "It is what the learner says and does that creates learning, not what the teacher says and does."

There was a time when the place of education in society, the authority of the institution, and the power of the individual teacher meant that coercion was enough to guarantee student cooperation. But there never was a golden age! Authoritarian control, coercion, and the self-evident value of education are no longer useful tools for the classroom practitioner.

Teachers have never been more challenged by the students in their care than the present generation is. At the same time they have never responded so professionally and with such energy. Teachers work hard. Perhaps they work harder than the students. It is our hope—and our experience—that using the methods we describe as Accelerated Learning do not require teachers to work any harder but, given the changing demands modern students place on them, to work much smarter.

The methods described in this book work most effectively when there is a shared understanding between teacher and student as to what learning involves, what processes are used, and what benefits are gained. Just because we have taught something does not mean that our students have understood it. In fact if we think they have, we may have fallen into the "teaching is performance" trap. Learning is not a spectator sport. Knowledge is not something that students passively absorb but something they create so that they can understand and apply it. It is what the learner says and does and thinks that creates learning, not what the teacher says and does and thinks.

This idea is at the heart of Accelerated Learning, which engages and involves students and is done with them and by them, and not simply to them. That is why they—not the teachers—should be exhausted at the end of the school year! After all, we are accelerating their learning.

> "The teacher is the architect of learning."

Now this new emphasis on learning and the learner does not fall into the trap of downplaying the role of the teacher. In fact the role of the teacher is much broader than merely "performing." The teacher is introducing and organizing the learning, making it emotionally safe to try, giving feedback, encouraging, probing with questions, and managing the experience throughout. In this role, the teacher is the architect of learning, not the one who delivers cement, sand, water, and bricks.

In this book we have tried to go beyond rhetoric and ground the Accelerated Learning model in four ways: We provide (1) a tried-and tested-model, (2) its theoretical underpinnings, (3) practical strategies, and (4) realistic solutions for teachers. You get model, theory, strategies, and solutions. What we are trying to do is to combine the art of teaching with the science of learning.

We like to think that some of our work refreshes the parts of teaching other learning theory has so far failed to reach, and it is for this reason that it has attracted so much general interest. In our view Accelerated Learning is not about drinking water, eating bananas, listening to Mozart, and taking brain breaks. It is about a structured, thought-through, and easily managed model for actively engaging learners in learning. It is highly self-conscious: Methods and outcomes are shared. It recognizes the importance of meeting the needs of the emotional curriculum while providing academic challenge. We embrace new technologies and say that they make an understanding of learning even more important for the teacher. The emerging technologies will not in themselves create better learners, but teachers who remain ignorant of their pervasive influence and liberating potential do so at their peril.

Creating the Learning Environment

Scaffold high cognitive challenge within low performance anxiety.

Focus on Learning

Share the language of learning.
Share the learning process.
Give constructive feedback.
Show concern for *improving* not *proving* performance.

Stay Positive and Purposeful

Share and explore high expectations.
Model the behaviors you want to see in students.
Distribute your interest equitably.
Believe that effort leads to success.

Connect to the Emotions

Structure individual, pair, and group work.
Provide opportunities for learners to express and explore emotions.
Balance criticism with praise.
Create an environment where students feel safe taking risks.

Adapt the Physical Space

Work to overcome limitations of heat, light, ventilation, and space.
Use visual displays to reinforce learning.
Include structured physical breaks.
Use movement to reinforce learning.

Questions to Ask Yourself

You only understand information relative to what you already understand.

As a teacher do you . . .

- focus on learning?
- involve everyone?
- use variety?
- explain your intent as you go?
- gear levels of difficulty to individual students?

Questioning Activities

- Ask open-ended questions.
- Seek descriptions, reflections, and speculations.
- Build in "think time" then "talk time" before asking for class responses.
- Use visual prompts, such as vocabulary linked to and organized around learning posters. (A learning poster summarizes essential content.)
- Have students ask questions and share information in pairs and small groups.
- Use thinking templates.
- Demonstrate answering exam questions.

As a teacher do you . . .

- focus on *improving* not *proving*?
- involve the learner?
- give specific feedback on ways to improve?
- ensure your feedback can be acted on?
- limit the amount of grading you do?

Feedback Activities

- Replace scores with improvement data.
- Use peer grading and peer teaching in ability groups.
- Use grades sparingly. Keep the emphasis on giving specific feedback for improvement. An emphasis on grades undermines other feedback systems.
- Have learners record your comments separately for purposes of revision and review.
- Share assessment criteria in learner-friendly language.
- Identify incremental improvements.
- Drop the word *ability*—replace it with *abilities*.
- Abandon effort grades.

What Do Your Students Think?
Student Questionnaire

It's what the learner says and does that creates learning, not what the teacher says and does.

In our learning . . .	Often	Sometimes	Never
We start by reviewing what we learned last lesson and what we already know about the topic.			
We agree on the learning goals and know what processes we will use to measure them.			
The learning goals are written where we can see them throughout the lesson.			
The classroom is a friendly place to be in.			
We are praised more than we are criticized.			
Our work is displayed in order to help our learning.			
The teacher is very positive			
There is space in the classroom to do different things; for example, reading, computer-based learning, and so on.			
We get up and move about periodically.			
We take an active part in discussions.			
The teacher presents new information to us using pictures and diagrams.			
Time goes by quickly.			
We are made to think.			
Our teacher uses lots of different ways to help us learn.			
We work in groups.			
Our teacher knows whether we have understood the lesson.			
We are encouraged to ask questions.			
We are encouraged to ask questions of other students.			
We get feedback on our progress during the lesson.			
We get a chance to reflect on *how* we have learned not just *what* we have learned.			

Accelerated Learning: A User's Guide ©2005 Crown House Publishing Ltd.

Motivating Learners

All meaningful learning involves risk.
Teachers help learners negotiate risk.

Belief in Ability Influences Ability

As a teacher you are the principal influencer in a classroom. You are communicating your expectations 100 percent of the time. Learners take their perceptions of their classroom abilities from you. Teacher belief shapes learner belief. You cannot teach students to believe in themselves, but you can develop self-confidence. Here is how.

BASICS: The Six Classroom Components of Self-Esteem

1. **B**elonging. Learners want to feel part of the shared experience—involve them.

2. **A**spiration. Learners want to know they can improve their worth—sell the benefits.

3. **S**afety. Learners want to know they are free from intimidation and humiliation—make your classroom a safe place to be. Make it a "no put-down" zone.

4. **I**dentity. Learners want to know they are recognized—value their individuality.

5. **C**hallenge. Learners need to be stretched—extend their comfort zones.

6. **S**uccess. Learners want the satisfaction of success—catch them improving.

How to Develop Self-Esteem

○ **Build from the BASICS.**
Restructure your everyday practice to follow the BASICS.

○ **Esteem the learner.**
Nurture positive relationships.

○ **Provide self-esteem-building experiences.**
Help learners negotiate risk.

○ **Reframe limiting beliefs.**
Help students interpret their experiences within a positive frame.

○ **Be clear, be coherent, be consistent, be confident!**

Principles of Accelerated Learning

Be expedient in strategy and consistent in principles.

The Accelerated Learning model is based on the following key principles. Our approach recognizes that it is important to be flexible, but the choices we make when designing learning experiences spring from a set of well-tested principles. This allows us to be both consistent and coherent in how we operate.

We Believe That Learning Is . . .

Connected	Learning is about seeking and securing connections.
Evolving	Learning evolves through exploration, imitation, and rehearsal.
Beneficial	Learning occurs when students can see the benefits of learning for themselves.
Negotiated	Learning occurs when we scaffold high cognitive challenge and negotiate risk.
Achievable	Learning requires optimism about achievable learner goals.
Sensory	Learning occurs through the senses.
Socially constructed	Learning is socially constructed with language as its medium.
Reflective	Learning thrives on immediate performance feedback and space for reflection.
Complex	Learning benefits from the attitude that intelligence is neither fixed nor inherited but complex, modifiable, and multiple.
Active	Learning involves the active engagement of various memory systems.
Rehearsed	Learning requires rehearsal in a variety of situations.

What the Principles of Accelerated Learning Mean

Learning is not a spectator sport.

We apply the key principles of Accelerated Learning in such a way as to . . .

- encourage learners actively to seek ways of connecting their learning to previous learning experiences, their present and future lives, the communities around them, and their own capabilities as learners. We seek and secure examples and applications that they can relate to and derive meaning from.
- understand that exploration, imitation, and rehearsal are natural ways to learn.
- sell the benefits of learning (the "What's in It for Me?" principle).
- scaffold high cognitive challenge and share the learning processes to help learners negotiate risk.
- work toward positive learner goals and encourage learners to share and reflect on their journey toward those goals.
- create very deliberate, carefully structured multisensory learning experiences.
- provide lots of opportunities for structured language exchange.
- give immediate performance feedback that students can act on right away, then provide space for reflection about content, process, and transferability.
- operate from the belief that intelligence is neither fixed nor inherited but capable of modification and development over a lifetime.
- adopt a sophisticated model of memory systems to make the learning experience individual and distinctive.
- use sophisticated techniques for review and reflection.

As described in chapter 2, we use a four-stage planning cycle to put these principles into an effective teaching process.

Accelerated Learning: The Learning Cycle

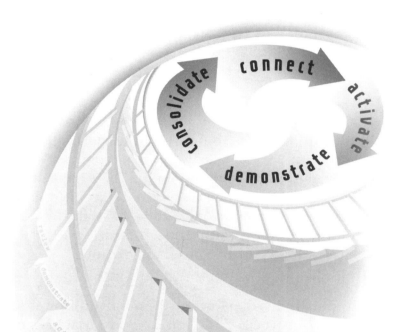

In Chapter 2 You Will Find

- ▶ Development of the Accelerated Learning Cycle
- ▶ Summary of the Accelerated Learning Cycle
- ▶ Connection Phase Activities
- ▶ Activation Phase Activities
- ▶ Demonstration Phase Activities
- ▶ Consolidation Phase Activities

Development of the Accelerated Learning Cycle

We shall not cease from our exploration, and the end
of all our exploring will be to arrive where we started
and to know the place for the first time.

—T. S. Eliot

In this book we advocate a four-stage cycle for engaging learners in learning. The cycle emphasizes learning and the learner rather than teaching and the teacher. Important features of our Accelerated Learning approach are that it is engaging, active, and reflective for both learner and teacher. The four-stage cycle is an affirmation of these features.

Models of Learning

Adopting a model of learning promotes thinking about learning. We argue throughout this book that self-awareness is important in order for learners to make sense of and articulate their learning experiences. We argue that both learner and teacher must make learning itself a focus of their thinking. At the end of the day, this exercise in self-awareness is not learning itself, nor is adopting one model out of many a recognition of the complexity and messiness of learning. However, adopting a model does provide a mechanism for constructing a language of learning as well as a focus for dialogue about learning.

Learning models are just that: models. They are not how people learn. They cluster around the pattern-making tendencies of humans and so are described as progressions, phases, constructs, lines, spirals, grids, triangles, or cycles. These are all metaphors that help us to retain the concepts and to make quick sense of them. Learning is a complex, messy, individual, and constructed experience that cannot be reduced by this or any other model to one compelling metaphor. Yet the Accelerated Learning Cycle does provides a set of reference points to help teacher and learner co-construct a critique of learning. The devil is in the details. For each stage in the cycle, we provide a set of pointers or prompts to shape your thinking.

A cycle—defined as a repeating series of occurrences—is a construct and thus a way of making sense of things. We hope it can be used to promote conversations that ultimately lead learners back, through learning, to themselves. The teacher facilitates and the cycle provides the tool.

Origins of the Accelerated Learning Cycle

Wisdom is meaningless until our own experience has given it meaning . . . and there is wisdom in the selection of wisdom.
—Bergen Evans

Our initial development of the Accelerated Learning Cycle owed a great deal to the work of those in the field of experiential learning, especially David Kolb and Kurt Lewin (see Kolb 1984; Lewin and Gold 1999). We attempted to recognize the importance of environments—both emotional and physical—and so acknowledged the work of Rita and Kenneth Dunn (1978). Later, the advent of emotional literacy seemed to further support our advocacy of a positive, supportive, and challenging environment for learning (see, for example, Goleman 1996).

Our early thinking explored concepts of brain laterality and so led us to the work of Bernice McCarthy and Ned Hermann (see, for example, Hermann 1997; McCarthy 1982). Richard Bandler and Michael Grinder, from the parallel universe of neurolinguistic processing, provided a practical rationale for structuring active engagement through VAK (visual, auditory, and kinesthetic processing; see, for example, Bandler 1992; Grinder 1991). Howard Gardner's (1993) promotion of a different view of intelligence and how it is measured provided a mechanism for our students to demonstrate their varieties of understandings. Popular texts on memory function and tools for improving memory helped with the detail of consolidating "knowing."

As we worked on the cycle, we promoted the ideas of scaffolding challenge, moving to the edge of personal comfort zones, and having the teacher facilitate this safely. Two very different influences played a part—Lev Vygotsky (1978) and the idea of proximal development, and Robert Sapolsky (1998), a primatologist, and his explanations of the true impact of stress on performance. Behind all this was the work of a loose band of eclectic thinkers from around the world, many of them members of what was then known as SALT (Society for Accelerated Learning Trainers), inspired by Georgi Lozanov (1978, 1981), and whose work Colin Rose captured in his Accelerated Learning books for adult learners (see, for example, Rose and Nicholl 1997). We created a very simple seven-stage Accelerated Learning Cycle and promoted it in a series of books and workshops. We advocated sharing the seven-stage Accelerated Learning Cycle, promoting it, using it as a framework for observations, and using it as a template for writing work, lesson, and unit plans. It took off!

Revisions to the Original Cycle

> *There are no shortcuts to any place worth going.*
> *—Beverley Sills*

We had three reasons for revising the cycle.

Emphasis. To focus on the learning and the learner rather than teaching and the teacher. Some of our thinking had been hijacked by those who mistakenly saw the cycle as all about teacher performance and caricatured it as a set of imaginative tools. We wish to affirm again the centrality of the learner.

Accessibility. Consolidating the original seven stages under four generic headings makes it easier for learner and teacher to share dialogue about learning.

Alignment. We feel that many current learning initiatives and the thinking behind them can be accommodated within this four-stage cycle. For example, the cognitive acceleration approach requires cognitive dissonance, social constructivism, metacognitive reflection, and transfer. We feel that these valuable components are inherent in our cycle.

The original Accelerated Learning Cycle had three steps that were all about orienting the learner to learning:

1. Connect the learning
2. Big picture
3. Describe the outcomes

We describe these three steps as the *Connection phase.*

The original Accelerated Learning Cycle had two steps concerned with engaging the learners and involving them in sense making:

4. Input
5. Activate

We describe these two steps as the *Activation phase.*

In the original Accelerated Learning Cycle step 6 provided opportunities for learners to show what they know.

6. Demonstrate

This step remains unchanged.

In the original seven-stage Accelerated Learning Cycle, step 7 provided opportunities for learners to test their learning through meaningful review.

7. Review

We describe this as the *Consolidation phase.*

So the four-stage Accelerated Learning Cycle looks like this:

1. **Connection** (including Connecting the Learning, Big Picture, and Outcomes)
2. **Activation** (including Input and Activate)
3. **Demonstration**
4. **Consolidation** (Review)

Summary of the Accelerated Learning Cycle

Make learning a focus of learning for it to endure.

Connection Phase
Do I connect to
- the content?
- the processes?
- the learners themselves?

Consolidation Phase
Do I
- structure active reflection on content and process?
- seek transfer?
- review then preview?

Activation Phase
Do I
- pose problems?
- use a multisensory approach?
- add language to doing?

Demonstration Phase
Do I
- use constructive feedback?
- vary groupings?
- offer multiple ways of demonstrating understanding?

Connection

Make learning personal. Start by connecting to what students have learned before and what they already know. Actively involve individuals, pairs, and groups. Manage the emotional climate so that no individual or group feels excluded. Agree on the big picture of content and process: "This is what we will do; this is how we will do it." Sell the benefits of learning. Make learning a focus of learning.

Activation

Give students the necessary information to begin to solve the problems you posed. Use problems, case studies, role-plays, props, stories, or visual or electronic aids in presenting information. Encourage learners to experience through seeing, hearing, and doing (VAK). Immerse activities in structured language exchange. Provide ongoing opportunities for description, reflection, and speculation. Give learners the opportunity to construct their own meanings in a variety of group situations (see "Great Ways to Get into Groups," pages 63–64).

Demonstration

Provide opportunities for learners to "show what they know" through several rehearsals and in multiple modes. Allow students to share their learning in a variety of groupings. Provide constructive feedback during or soon after the real experience. Place the emphasis of your feedback on improving not "proving." Give specific advice about process and content improvement that students can act on straight away.

Consolidation

Reflect on what has been learned and how. Combine paired, small-group, and whole-class activities. Link to the process and content goals shared in the Connection phase. Then address transfer: How could what we have learned be useful elsewhere? Preview what will come in the next lesson.

Connection Phase Activities

We only understand information relative to what we already know.

The Connection phase should help students to access and understand the links between separate learning experiences. This phase helps students to remember previous learning—what they did and why—as well as draw out what they already know about a topic. The Connection phase also helps students pose questions about the relevance of the learning: What would be useful to know? This is also an important opportunity to share learning goals with students and to agree on success criteria.

Agreeing on the Learning Goals

Some teachers may prefer to connect the learning or engage the learner before agreeing on the learning goals. Yet at some point in the Connection phase it is important to agree on the learning goals with students. This can occur in a variety of imaginative and involving ways, some of which follow.

When planning a lesson ask yourself beforehand, "What will my students have learned and be able to do by the end of my lesson that they could not do before?" This is a good way of focusing on what your real learning goals are. For example,

> *"By the end of this lesson, we will be able to confidently discuss reasons why the Berlin Wall was built from the perspectives of both East and West"*

is a clear learning goal. Whereas,

> *"Today we will study the Berlin Wall"*

is not even a learning goal but a description of what you will be doing.

Involve your students in deciding what would be good learning goals:

> *"Before we start this new topic, what do we already know about it? What would be good to know about it? How should we go about finding out?"*

Also consider how the learning is stretching your students; relate the agreed on learning goals to Bloom's (1956) taxonomy of thinking as shown in the figure on page 22. Encourage your students to do the same as they discuss what their individual and collective learning goals could be.

Consider the following learning goals:

> *"By the end of this lesson we will be able to recall three examples of sedimentary rock."*

This goal is clearly knowledge based and represents the lowest rung on Bloom's thinking hierarchy. The following goal falls within the next level of thinking, comprehension:

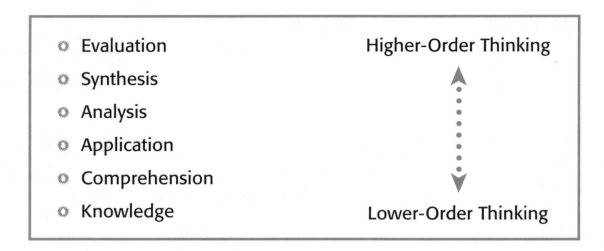

"We will also be able to explain how metamorphic rock is formed."

Finally, the following is clearly a higher-order thinking skill:

"We will compare and contrast the rock cycle to the water cycle."

As a teacher you might decide to differentiate the learning goals thus. Everyone will be able recall three examples of each type of rock—sedimentary, metamorphic, and igneous. Most will be able to explain how metamorphic rocks are formed. Some will be able to compare and contrast the rock cycle to the water cycle. You may wish to distinguish between learning goals at different levels by using the descriptors *must, should,* and *could*. As a general principle, brief and debrief process and content outcomes and do so with the active involvement of the students.

> Help students to access and understand the links between separate learning experiences.

You may want all your students to be able to do all these things. Be aware of how your learning goals relate to thinking. Without deliberation most learning goals involve students simply repeating or recalling information. This is the lowest level of thinking: knowledge.

Use a thinking wall, which could be a space where you can display question prompts and where students can place answers written on sticky notes alongside, or could be a display of Bloom's taxonomy surrounded by key words related to thinking in order to help develop a "thinking" vocabulary with your students. Ask students to pole-bridge their level of thinking and to use the terms described on the thinking wall to help them. *Pole-bridging,* a term coined by Win Wenger (see, for example, Wenger and Poe 1996), involves techniques that integrate the different areas, or poles, of the brain, particularly through sensory techniques. Pole-bridging requires learners to articulate their thinking aloud while undertaking a learning activity and consequently helps them to better understand their thinking.

Agree on What Success Will Look Like, Sound Like, and Feel Like

Make clear your success criteria. Involve students in setting their own. Ask them, "If you are really successful in this lesson, what will you be able to do, say, or talk about by the end of it?" Have them write their success criteria on a large sheet of chart paper and pin it up in the classroom where it can be seen and referred to throughout the lesson.

In some instances you may want to pose a problem without first clarifying the learning goals. This deliberate use of what some call cognitive dissonance ought not to come as a sudden challenge, but should be situated within the students' understanding of your purpose of facilitating real learning. So share the process: "We are going to pose a problem in order to develop a different thinking approach" is better than "Here's the problem. What do you think?"

Here are activities to connect learning on a personal level.

1. Break a Pattern

Do something that arrests attention and challenges expectations! But be careful when you do so. For example, a math teacher introduced his students to rational and irrational numbers by giving each student in his class either a blue card or a red card. He placed one upside down on each student's desk. On each card was written either a rational number (whole number or integer) or an irrational number (for example, the square root of two or a never-ending decimal). He then asked all the students with blue cards to stand at one side of the classroom and all those with red cards to stand at the other side. Unnoticed by the students all the boys had blue cards (rational numbers) and all the girls had red cards (irrational numbers).

He then went on to explain that irrational numbers were like women in that they went "on and on and on, often without making any sense," whereas rational numbers were like men: "clear, concise, and to the point." You can imagine the uproar in the classroom as the girls responded that perhaps rational numbers were like men in that they were "simple." It was a great way to hook the students emotionally and one that his students never forgot. We must point out that he obviously did not mean any of his sexist comments to be taken seriously, and he explained to his students why he had made them at the end of the lesson!

2. Create a Sense of Anticipation

A French teacher might don a customs officer's cap and collect passports at her classroom door because the students are now entering France. A math teacher might start her lesson with a mind-reading trick based on algebraic equations, or a history teacher might hand out propaganda leaflets to students as they enter his classroom.

3. Powerful PowerPoint

Create a scrolling PowerPoint presentation of images connected to the topic. Ask students to view the presentation and to guess what topic they are going to study.

4. Contextualizing Music

Play music as students enter the classroom. This music could be linked to the topic; for example, the theme to *Star Wars* played at the beginning of a lesson about forces—"May the force be with you" – or the theme to *M.A.S.H.* at the beginning of a history lesson about the Korean Conflict.

5. Imagine

Ask students to place themselves in a situation; for example, to imagine they live in a world without electricity. They must describe in words, pictures, or both their journey to school from the moment they wake up.

Here are activities to help students connect to previous learning.

1. Vocabulary Search

Here's a really easy way to get students thinking about the previous lesson that is also fun and will back up your school's literacy strategy. Choose seven key words from the previous lesson and jumble up the letters. Students work with partners to unscramble the words and solve the key word mystery. Try these:

netcnoc

het

gaelninr

2. Ranking

Have students break into groups. Give each group a set of nine statements relating to the previous week's learning. They have to organize the statements into *A-*, *B-*, and *C-*level priorities according to established criteria. This allows them to rank certain statements as equal in importance.

3. Early Starters

Put some review questions on the board so students entering the room can get started on them right away. For the super-organized, prime this activity by introducing the questions at the close of the previous day or previous lesson.

4. Whiteboard Snowstorm

Give each student a sticky note as he or she enters the room. Ask students to write down the three most important things they think they learned in the last lesson; they have about three minutes to do this and can refer to their notes or talk to a partner. After three minutes ask them to come up and stick their notes on the board. Hey, presto! Three minutes into the lesson you have a "blizzard" of pieces of paper outlining what the students think are the most important things they have learned. Summarize a number of these, making sure that you emphasize what you think were the important points (recall is dramatically improved with review). You can now start the lesson.

5. Question Wall

A question wall is a bulletin board or other display area set aside for students to attach sticky-note questions to. The exercise is similar to that in the preceding activity, but this time students write two important questions they still have about the previous lesson. You can start your lesson by answering a number of questions, taking the opportunity to clear up any fundamental misunderstandings.

6. 1 3 5 7

All students write down one thing they remember from last week, then share their items with a partner to see if they can agree on three things. Next in a small group they agree on five, and finally as a class try to agree on seven.

7. Key Vocabulary and Definitions

Divide students into groups of four and give each group an envelope containing ten key vocabulary words from previous lessons or topics and separate definitions on pieces of paper. Each group must reach a consensus on the correct definition for each word and place the definition next to the key word on the desk in front of them.

Here are activities to connect to learning to come.

1. Visual Cues

Provide a blank flow chart labeled with key vocabulary from the topic. Students fill in the flow chart after each lesson by adding three things they have learned in each box.

Another activity is Big Pictures: Post ten images that summarize key pieces of learning about the whole topic around the room. Ask students to visit this "gallery" of pictures and to discuss each picture in turn.

Create a glossary of key vocabulary in alphabetical order and ask students to add to it during each lesson.

2. Mapping

Give students a memory-mapped overview of the whole topic, and during each lesson have them shade in or tick the learning goal of that lesson.

Give students a module map (literally a map of the whole topic showing the way through from beginning to end) at the beginning of a topic.

Make a set of learning mats—laminated 11" x 17" sheets containing key words and images—for students to use as desk protectors. They put their textbooks on top of the desk protectors while they are working but can always check where they are in the topic. They can also write on these sheets with dry-erase markers.

3. Artifact or Prop

This is an activity for individuals, pairs, or groups. Select and bring in to class an artifact or prop that relates to the day's lesson or a new topic. Introduce the item and explain the connections. Better still, ask students to guess what the prop has to do with the forthcoming lesson. For the greatest effectiveness, provide processing time before students guess the connections. Bring in the artifacts the week before and make a general statement about them: "Next week we will be discovering the significance of these items for your grandparents." Display the set of items at the front of the room.

4. Learning to Learn Checklist

Students work in groups to devise a checklist of different ways of learning. They summarize their findings on flip chart paper or the like, and then collate the findings as a class activity. The final list provides a learning to learn checklist for them to use during and at the end of a unit.

5. What Happens Next?

Get students to predict what comes next. For example, in a music lesson, play the first part of a song, then press the pause button and ask the students to sing what comes next. Or in an English lesson, write the first three lines of a verse of poetry on the board and deliberately leave the fourth line blank. Ask students to work in pairs to come up with a fourth line before revealing what the poet wrote.

6. The Axis of Learning

This activity is suggested by Paul Ginnis (2005). Affix a large cross to the floor with masking tape. Label one end of the horizontal axis "I know a lot," the other, "I know nothing." Ask students to position themselves on the point that reflects their knowledge of the topic. Now label one end of the vertical axis "I want to know a lot," the other "I want to know nothing." Students then position themselves according to their level of interest in the topic. Completing this activity allows you to pose lots of questions about learning and its relevance to individual students. It also provides a review tool at the end of the lesson.

7. Art Gallery

At the beginning of a topic set up an "art gallery" of laminated images or statements about the topic to be studied; for example, images from World War II with newspaper headlines from that time, or scenes and quotations from a play to be studied. As students enter the classroom, play classical (art gallery) music and invite them to stroll in pairs around the gallery. Explain that in five minutes' time they must choose an image or statement that touches a chord (makes a connection) with them, and when the music stops, they must go and stand next to it and be prepared to justify their decision. This provides an engaging and different start to a lesson and also has the advantage of creating a ready-made and relevant display that you can refer to throughout the lesson.

Activation Phase Activities

There is little point in giving students ready-made meaning.
—Paul Ginnis

The Activation phase should help students become familiar with the key information they need to solve a problem, hypothesize, or simply remember something that is essential. The information should be conveyed in ways that are multisensory, elicit questions, and engage curiosity. In the Activation phase students become directly engaged with the problem presented. Use any combination of the following activities to activate learning.

1. Choose It

Include opportunities for students to make choices within your lesson—choice is a huge motivator. Recognize that students learn in different ways. For example, divide your room into a "practical" zone and a "research" zone and allow the students to choose the zone in which they want to learn.

In one school where tenth-grade science was taught at the same time in four adjoining rooms, the teachers created four different learning zones based on Howard Gardner's (1993) multiple intelligence theory and allowed students to choose which room to work in. Surprisingly, students did not just follow their friends—especially when the reasons for setting up these learning environments were explained to them.

2. Multisensory Immersion

Imagine this . . .

You walk into a classroom where a large video-projected picture of a volcano erupting fills a screen. Students watch as molten magma shoots hundreds of feet into the air. Chunks of rock, some pieces the size of buses, crash from the sky.

As they watch, students pass around pieces of igneous rock (granite and basalt), feeling the weight and texture of each rock for a few moments before handing it on to the next student. In the corner of the lab, a piece of sulfur is heating, releasing a sulfurous odor into the room. The roar of the exploding volcano is almost deafening. As the short video clip comes to an end, the teacher displays the rock cycle. She explains that the rocks in their hands come from that volcano and invites the class to join her on a journey around the rock cycle: "Imagine you are that piece of rock. Feel the heat as you run in molten form down the mountainside."

This introduction to the core content of the lesson is multisensory and memorable because students see, hear, feel, and smell in an immersion-learning experience.

This is your opportunity to create a dynamic and unforgettable experience for your students. Hook them into the lesson. The teacher in the volcano example might further hook students into the lesson and make it relevant to them by explaining, "The only thing between us and all that molten lava is about thirty miles of the Earth's crust." Make the presentation unusual or dramatic (people remember dramatic, emotional events).

Also make your presentation reasonably short—no more than ten or fifteen minutes. Remember, the enemy of learning is the talking teacher. Ask yourself, "If I knew nothing about this topic and had just been given this information, would moving through this activity really lead me to a deeper understanding?"

3. Uncoverage, or Reveal It!

Place a picture related to the topic on an overhead projector, using two cards to cover all but a small part of the picture. Ask students what they think the picture shows. Then reveal more of the picture and ask the students if they have changed their minds. Continue doing this as more and more of the whole picture is revealed.

4. Piece It Together

Cut a page of written information into sections. Put the sections into envelopes and give them out to the students. Working in pairs, the students piece the sections back together in the right order so that the information makes sense.

5. Label It

Take a labeled diagram from a textbook and photocopy it without the labels so that you are left with just the picture. Ask the students to discuss what they think the diagram shows and to add their own labels.

6. Real-Life Challenge

Present the topic in the context of a real-life situation or problem to be solved. For example, "How can we ensure that everyone on the planet has access to fresh water? You are a team of experts brought in to advise the U.S. government on a series of emergency measures for dealing with drought conditions."

Or present a cross-age tutoring scenario; for example, "You have been asked to prepare a lesson to teach middle-school students the chemistry of salt. What will they need to know? How will you explain quite complex ideas in simple language? Remember you will also need to present the information in an interesting way to hold their attention."

7. Home and Away Groups

Moving in and out of groups is made easier when you play Home and Away. Home groups are friendship groups. Away groups are teacher-directed, non-friendship groups. Just like sports teams, students expect to play at home and away. For example, students might start in their home groups to develop an action plan for a project, then move into expert groups to research a topic, before returning to their home groups to share what they have learned.

8. Thinking Prompts or Templates

Use laminated sets of prompt sheets to develop thinking. Individualize them. Use them for individual and group use. David Hyerle's (2000) thinking maps provide a useful selection of tools to help students analyze information.

9. Self-Talk

Remind students, "Talk yourself through it as you do it!" Bridge the left and right hemispheres of the brain by insisting that students deliberately and slowly talk themselves through an activity. Encourage them to use relevant vocabulary. Isolate examples of "good noticing"—such as when a student has completed a science experiment and correctly labeled all the phenomena noticed. Use Self-Talk with any activity that involves a physical sequence. For example, students might explain a Mind Map out loud while simultaneously tracing the connections between ideas with their fingers.

10. Roving Reporter

The reporter wanders around, microphone in hand, interviewing individuals or groups about their progress on a particular task. Every now and again you pause the task and have the reporter report back to the class. This provides a form of review and a means of checking understanding, prompting participation, and keeping students on track.

11. Get Physical!

Help students to associate physical movement with content to develop understanding and link to muscle, or procedural, memory (see page 43). For example, in a German lesson, students say the phrase, "Ich wache auf" (I wake up) at the same time as they mime a stretching motion as if just waking up. Or, in a science lesson, students say out loud, "Transpiration is about plants getting important minerals from the ground" while miming digging those important minerals out of the ground. In order to provoke more thought, get students to mime more abstract concepts, such as stages of the water cycle or perhaps their physical interpretation of the Treaty of Versailles.

12. Video Conferencing

Video conferencing is a useful way of exchanging relevant information between two schools or other locations. It is also a useful way of interviewing an expert or someone role-playing an expert. Set up a panel of inquiry. We all behave differently in front of a camera!

13. Electronic Whiteboard or Computer Projection

Use a projector hooked up to a computer or an electronic whiteboard (if you are lucky enough to have one) for a variety of purposes:

- **Displaying stunning visuals.** Use Google image search to find relevant pictures.
- **Turning your classroom into a movie theater.** Make sure you have quality speakers attached if you use a projection screen or whiteboard.
- **Downloading online video.** You can use Google to search for relevant clips.
- **Creating drag-and-drop exercises** in which students match key vocabulary to images.
- **Displaying a skeleton concept map.** Create a concept map using Inspiration software and have students add to it.
- **Taking digital photos.** Photograph students' work in progress and display it throughout the lesson.
- **Displaying "electronic ticker" messages.** Flash key messages across the screen throughout the lesson.
- **Using a "countdown clock"** to time activities.
- **Encouraging students to discuss ideas and practice presentations.** Hey, teacher, let the students use the hardware!

Also see section on using communication technology to underpin Accelerated Learning (pages 74–77).

14. Re-creation Recreation!

On an 11" x 17" piece of paper, represent the new information the students need to know using words and images, preferably including color. Place this paper, covered, at the front of the classroom (for example, at your desk). Students work in teams of four. Each team has an 11" x 17" sheet of white paper and a selection of colored pens. Their challenge will be to re-create as accurately as possible the information on your paper. Group members count off from one to four. Call up the number ones, who have one minute to come to the front of the class and study the information. They return to their groups and relate what they saw. The group scribe then has to record this information on the group's sheet of paper. Next call up the number twos for one minute, then the threes, then the fours. If group members are collaborating, they will work out a plan to help them get all the information by the fourth trip to the front; for example, "Number two, you get information from the top right-hand corner," and so on.

15. Carousel

Set up three information stations in the room related to the current topic. The first station has a tape recording of a spoken conversation, the second contains a TV and VCR, and the third contains relevant magazines and articles. Divide your class into three groups. Each group spends ten minutes at each station before moving on to the next one. You can use a related piece of music as a cue when it is time to move on.

16. Matching

Give students envelopes containing equal numbers of cutout statements and pictures. They work in pairs or groups of four to match the statements to the pictures. You can also do this activity with key vocabulary and definitions. The exercise is visual because it contains images, auditory because students discuss their choices, and kinesthetic (physical) because students physically arrange the information on the table in front of them.

17. Active Concert

This is a technique from suggestopedia, which derives from the work of Georgi Lozanov (1981), a Bulgarian linguist who emphasizes the importance of a state of relaxed alertness. Prepare a script that tells about the key information in the form of a story. Include all the essential vocabulary. Read the script aloud to the class to a musical accompaniment. The second time around, have members of the class read parts in turn.

18. Nested Learning within a Story

This technique involves introducing learning points, key concepts, and vocabulary indirectly. Hidden within the story are all the elements the learner needs. For example, the story could be about the planets but without using the word *planet* and instead describing an exaggerated tale about Pluto, Neptune, Mars, and so on. You tell the story, then come back to it later during the lesson.

Demonstration Phase Activities

If you understand it, you can explain it.
—Albert Einstein

The Demonstration phase forms a loop with the A_____ ___hase. In the Demonstration phase students are given opportunities to generate products that demonstrate their understanding. They can also convey their understanding through written or spoken exchanges. The learner's thinking is fine-tuned through feedback from the teacher or other students in the class. The Demonstration phase is highly interactive, rich in opportunities for constructive feedback, and student centered. Use any combination of the following activities to have students demonstrate their learning.

1. Explain It to Someone Else

Real understanding involves transfer of knowledge to a different context. Having taught what you thought was the best lesson of your life, you discover the importance of "show what you know." Imagine a lesson on particles of matter presented to a very proficient class. You take students through a sequence of animated images showing exactly what happens to the particles in ice as an ice cube melts to become water and then boils to become steam. You combine this with the "states of matter body bop," in which students move their hands to simulate the movement of particles in a solid, liquid, and gas. You then ask the class to imagine they are a particle in a lump of wax and to describe what happens as the wax is gently heated. One girl stares hard at her book for a couple of minutes before saying, "I can't do this." When you ask her why not she replies, "Because now you want to know about wax when you've only taught us about water."

Learners have difficulty transferring understanding and applying it to slightly different contexts. Without the Demonstration part of the cycle, this difficulty does not get exposed. When you are thinking of activities to allow students to show what they have learned, it is probably worth remembering the old saying attributed to Albert Einstein: "You haven't really understood it unless you can explain it to someone else." So get your students to explain their new understanding to each other.

2. Hot Seating

A student acting as the expert sits in the hot seat. Try having the student take on the persona of a president; a beam of light; Alexander the Great; a World War I poet; or the inventor of the pop-up toaster, the cell phone, or the soap bubble! The student answers the questions in that role.

3. Web Page

A student or group of students designs a web page (or just the plan for one) with all the appropriate features to share their learning. Use an $8^1/_2$" x 11" paper template to promote discussion about editing, navigation, and use of text and images. Older and more advanced students can actually upload their page to the Internet. (See tips on producing web pages in "Designing Accelerated Learning Web Pages," pages 79–80.)

4. Press Conference

Groups of students take turns presenting findings through a simulated press conference. The reporters ask questions and take notes in order to rush out a front-page scoop ahead of the competition.

5. Walk-Through

A walk-through is where students literally walk through the stages in a process. For example, you might label areas of your classroom as parts of the respiratory system and, pretending to be a blood cell, students walk through the heart, where they are pumped into the lungs to become oxygenated, and then back into the heart to be pumped around the body to the cells, where oxygen (a red card) is exchanged for carbon dioxide (a blue card), and so on. The students explain what is happening at each stage, or a single student acts as narrator.

6. Tableau

A group of students takes a scene from a book, play, or moment in history. They freeze into positions designed to convey a sense of what is going on, literally creating a frozen three-dimensional tableau. Other students can walk around the tableau and may "unfreeze" certain figures in it by tapping them on the shoulder. They can question the unfrozen figure, who must stay in his or her role, and then freeze the figure back into the tableau with another tap to the shoulder.

7. Freeze-Frame

A freeze-frame involves a walk-through that is deliberately stopped. Use freeze-frame to pause what students are doing, then ask questions (or get other students to ask questions): Who is doing what? Why? What happens next? and so on.

8. Mini Presentations

A group of students makes a short presentation to another group of students, who are allowed to ask questions. The "audience" group of students must give the presenting group feedback on how they might improve their presentation. The feedback is most effective if students are asked to comment only on specific aspects of the presentation; for example, clarity of explanation, use of diagrams, or the like.

9. PowerPoint

PowerPoint is a powerful, must-have piece of software. Students create their own PowerPoint presentations to show what they have learned to the rest of the class. They can even create a PowerPoint for review purposes that summarizes the main information within a topic. Other students can use this as a study resource.

10. Role-Play

Students role-play their understanding. They might act out the stages of the water cycle, the steps in solving a math problem, or the sequence of movements for shooting a layup in basketball. Including a narrator may make role-playing easier.

11. Puppet Show

This activity may seem a little childish, but even older students really enjoy it. Students use index cards, paper plates, and straws to make their own puppets and props and a labeled background. They then crouch behind a desk and perform to another group their understanding of, for example, French fashion (in French), the Cold War, or the water cycle. Saying thoughts out aloud is also a good pole-bridging, or brain integration, activity.

12. Storyboard or Cartoon Strip

Create a storyboard or cartoon strip to explain a process; for example, steps in an experiment or scenes from a book.

13. Group Presentation

As previously mentioned, Einstein said that if you understand something, you can explain it to somebody else. So get students in one group to present what they have learned to another group of students, who offer feedback and suggestions for improvement (see also "Smart Grading," pages 54–56).

14. Pop Sox, Vox Pops

These are quirky little radio interviews on a variety of issues, complete with sound effects and musical jingles. Give the students a cassette recorder and ask them to prepare a two-minute radio spot, presenting the most important aspects of what they have just learned. You can collect these to use as resources in other lessons.

15. Bazaar

Tell students that they will be transforming the classroom into a mini-market of knowledge and information. Working in groups of four, they are to set up "booths" around the classroom where they will display and sell their new understanding. Two of the group will staff the booth, while the other two can visit the other booths to see what they can bring back. After ten minutes they can swap places.

16. Beat the Examiner

Get students to create tests for each other. They must come up with questions they think an examiner might ask and must also prepare an answer key. They then swap and try to complete each others' "Beat the Examiner" tests. Tests are returned to the examiners for grading and feedback.

17. Bullet Point Summary

Students prepare a bulleted-list summary of the key information in the lesson. This list must be in the form of an "essential guide" that they offer as a learning resource for other students to use.

18. Artist's Easel

Each student receives a sheet of paper containing a couple of paragraphs of information on the topic being studied. On the same sheet of paper there is also a blank box in the shape of an artist's easel. They must do the following in sequence:

1. Work on their own (intrapersonal activity) to draw images, pictures, diagrams, stick figures, and so on, in the blank artist's easel to remind them of the important information contained in the paragraphs. The idea is that they make their own sense of the text-based information by constructing a visual interpretation.

2. They then pair/share with a partner, explaining to each other their images and what they mean (interpersonal activity).

3. Next they could use the same information, but this time, again working on their own, they select what they think are the seven most important key words and must be prepared to justify their choices (linguistic intelligence).

4. They arrange the seven key words in order of importance—the most important at the top, the least important at the bottom. Once again, they must be prepared to justify their ranking of the key words. Sequencing or ordering information taps in to the logical-mathematical intelligence.

5. Once again students can pair/share with a friend, comparing their words and the order of importance they have ranked them in, and justifying their decisions.

6. Finally, working with a friend, students must come up with a mime or physical action for each key word and be prepared to perform it in front of a small group of other students. The other students should be able to guess from the physical mime or movement which key word is being performed. In this step students are working in the kinesthetic, or physical, intelligence.

This activity can be easily individualized because the paragraphs the students start with can be as simple or as complex as you choose.

Consolidation Phase Activities

Learning without reviewing is like trying to fill the bath without putting the plug in.
—Mike Hughes

The Consolidation phase provides an opportunity for students to reflect on what they have learned and how. In the Consolidation phase, students focus on the content (what do we now know and understand that we did not before?) and the process (how have we learned and how can we apply our learning methods elsewhere?).

In the Consolidation phase students also get an opportunity to see the relevance of their learning to their own lives, as you draw examples of how the new learning can be applied in the world beyond the classroom. Finally, in the Consolidation phase you preview the learning to come. Use any combination of the following activities in the Consolidation phase.

1. An Uplifting Experience

Three students imagine they are in an elevator going up ten floors. It takes 90 seconds to travel ten floors. In that time, one student describes what has been accomplished, another reflects on how they did it and why, and the final person speculates about how the learning might be useful outside of school. Then they change roles.

2. Each One Teach One

In pairs, students answer these questions: What three things that are really important have you learned today? and What three processes have you used that have helped your learning? When the pair has agreed on their conclusions, they share them with another pair—perhaps this time trying to agree on five items.

3. Visitor from an Alien Planet

Students imagine they have to teach an alien from another planet what they have learned about a topic. Each lists one benefit, three facts, and five words the alien would need to know, then in a pair they practice teaching their list.

4. Pop Quizzes

Regularly review through the use of short but frequent pop quizzes. There are four types of quizzes: test yourself, test your partner, test the teacher, and teacher test the class. Of these, the most useful is the self-test. Encourage varied but frequent brief quizzes. Research shows that spaced, active testing significantly improves recall.

5. Team Maps

Place a graphic representation (such as a Mind Map) of key content at the front of the room. In groups of four, students reconstruct their own version of it. Each student comes up twice to the desk to study the map for ten seconds each, for a total of eight visits and eighty seconds. The students agree on a strategy for capturing the content beforehand and can refine their strategy before the final visit. They construct their map and then discuss their strategies. This brings out issues such as hierarchies, categories, main facts and details, connections, and prompts.

6. Review Poems

Use narrative verse or even a haiku to summarize some key learning. Individuals or groups read their learning poems aloud to the class.

7. Module Map

Students fill in and complete over time a map of the unit they are studying that shows the main concepts or ideas they need to understand. They can color-code each one to show their level of understanding; for example,

red = I need to look at this again.

yellow = I partially understand this.

green = I completely understand this.

Using this color scheme creates a "traffic lights" review.

8. Game Show Quiz

Who Wants to Be a Millionaire with generous prizes! Pictionary, whiteboard Scrabble, Jeopardy, and The Strongest Link are all favorites.

9. Video Journal

Groups of students record learning summaries on video. Divide the class into four groups and assign each a different area to focus on. When they review, they do so with the camera rolling. The recording then becomes a resource for future reference.

10. The Question Box

Students write their unanswered questions on folded slips of paper and put them in the box. You can then answer the questions directly or hand them out to groups to research and answer.

11. Interpretations

Different groups summarize the key information from the points of view of different historical characters. Examples could include an Egyptian construction worker from the time of pyramid building, a modern-day firefighter, a writer of children's stories, a football coach, a childcare worker, or a tabloid journalist. Students then compare their versions and discuss interpretations and bias. Alternatively, they might summarize the lesson in the style of a soap opera or "fly on the wall" documentary.

12. Review Races

Divide the class into three teams. Give each team a different colored marker (for example, green team, red team, blue team). Hang three flip chart–size pieces of paper at the front of the room. The rule is students can move only when they have been passed the marker. One student in each team takes the pen, goes to the chart paper, and writes one thing he or she has learned on the team's piece of paper. The student returns and passes the pen to the next member of the team. This person then goes up and writes something different he or she has learned, and so on. The winning team is the one with the greatest number of new things learned.

13. 3, 2, 1 Block Review

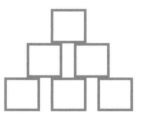

On sticky notes or in squares drawn on a sheet of paper, students write

one thing I already know,

two questions I still want to ask, and

the three most important things I have learned.

14. Passive Concert

This technique is derived from suggestopedia. While playing a piece of instrumental music with a steady fifty to sixty beats per minute, review the key information from a topic. Allow the students to listen to the music as you speak just below its volume. Take your time, breathe steadily, and use open-ended questions and nondirective language.

15. Make It into a Song

Take key information and set it to a popular tune. Try this one about the rock cycle set to the tune of "Frère Jacques."

> **Verse 1:** Metamorphic, metamorphic,
> Marble slate, marble slate
> Sedimentary limestone, sedimentary limestone
> Mudstone, shale, mudstone, shale
>
> **Verse 2:** Lava cooling, lava cooling
> Igneous, igneous
> Underground is granite, underground is granite
> Basalt on top, basalt on top.
> —*K. Brechin*

16. Circle Time Debrief

Rearrange the furniture so students are sitting in a circle. Debrief the lesson through the use of open-ended questions designed to draw out both the content of the lesson and the learning processes. For example,

○ How do we know we have been successful?
○ What worked well in this lesson?
○ What might we do differently next time?

Remember to allow thinking time and be prepared for students, especially secondary students, to get used to circle time.

17. Photographic Evidence

Take photographs of students at work and display them at the end of the lesson. This is a very powerful way of exploring learning processes with the students. For example, "Look at this group working together. How can we tell they are collaborating really effectively as a team?" Display the photos again in the next lesson to connect the learning and to help build a community of learners.

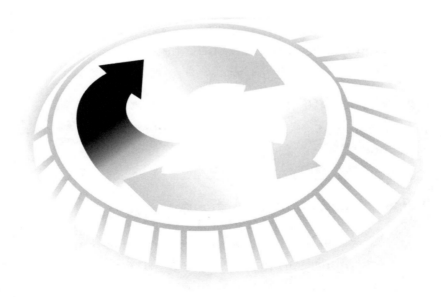

Accelerated Learning: Making Learning Memorable

In Chapter 3 You Will Find

▶ Memory and Learning

▶ Memory Models

Memory and Learning

Memory can be improved, though not perfected.

Imagine if you had a perfect memory. Your life would be hell! Memory is effective and healthy when we can leave what we deem to be irrelevant behind.

A good memory is necessary to perform well in the standardized tests through which we currently judge students' learning. Indeed some argue that the SAT and other standardized tests are predominantly memory tests. We can improve our own memory function through practicing memory techniques. We can improve student recall of learning by understanding how memory works and adapting our classroom practices accordingly. Here are some guidelines, derived from an understanding of memory function, on how to make classroom learning more memorable.

> 1. Use the three memory systems.
> 2. Prime through context.
> 3. Connect and chunk upward and downward.
> 4. Give significance to beginnings and endings.
> 5. Expect variance.
> 6. Use a variety of testing procedures to improve recall.
> 7. Use places, faces, and spaces.

Here are explanations of these guidelines with some examples of what they might mean for you as the teacher.

1. Use the Three Memory Systems

Researchers have identified different memory systems. By operating across the systems, you increase opportunities for recall.

Semantic memory involves facts, figures, and data. This memory system is highly vulnerable to loss, misinterpretation, and bias. The rote repetition of facts, figures, or information is unlikely to create enduring recall, but doing so in combination with a vivid or unusual context and perhaps a combination of physical movements might have a more lasting effect. A list of key events from the twentieth century learned by rote is less likely to endure than is the same information rehearsed through individual members of the class inventing a mime that captures each event, forming a line, and acting them out in order. The latter takes time, but the payoff is that the information sticks.

Episodic memory involves moments, events, and contexts. Once again, episodes are susceptible to false memory, misinterpretation, and bias. Knowing that unusual contexts, distinctive physical locations, and experiences with high emotional resonance all shape and enhance recall allows you to position distinctive episodes strategically. If students learn about the fertilization of a plant, not by reading their notes but by physically standing up and creating a human model of the sequence, it gets remembered.

Procedural memory involves sequences and what is known as muscle memory. If you play golf, you will know that your body does not always follow your mind! By practicing a bad swing again and again, it becomes part of motor, or muscle, memory. Your body aligns itself according to this learned imprint and to unlearn it becomes increasingly difficult. That's why some golfers, despite years of experience, reach a limit. Their swing has been learned to such a degree it's virtually impossible to break it back down again to correct the faults. A movement imprinted in the muscle resists forgetting. If you pair information with a series of complementary movements, you dramatically increase the chances of remembering it. For example teaching the numbers from one to twenty in French with an accompanying physical gesture for each number makes them more likely to be retained.

2. Prime through Context

You may have had the experience of remembering an event by prompting yourself, or being prompted, about the circumstances in which it occurred. For example, police are trained in questioning strategies that elicit information by defining the circumstances around which an event occurred. Having your students leave space for a running commentary in their note-taking will help prime recall. Have your older students learn how to record context and content in their notes. The emotional quality of an experience also shapes recall. With too much emotion, it is difficult to forget, too little and it does not hit the radar. When you review key information, try to do so in a way that provides a vivid context and an emotional resonance. The example of the key events from the twentieth century (described under semantic memory) works because it is individually involving, highly unusual, and thus memorable.

3. Connect and Chunk Upward and Downward

Humans retain information better when they can connect it to something familiar and when it comes in bite-size chunks. When you give information, do so in the smallest permissible number of chunks and with a number attached—for example, "five features of a glaciated valley." When you review, chunk upward by starting small and growing bigger: Name one key point from last week, now swap with a partner and agree on three points from last week, now in a group discuss and agree on five points from last week. For recall, the fewer chunks of information the better—five causes of World War I, three reasons for Hamlet's indecision—as long lists are difficult to access. A Mind Map is a particularly good mechanism for connecting and chunking.

4. Give Significance to Beginnings and Endings

Watch the national television news in the early evening. The news anchor previews the top stories at the beginning and reviews them at the end. Humans pay extra attention to what they perceive to be at the beginning and the ending of an experience. In learning have positive, directing beginnings and conclusive endings. Also include lots of little review opportunities—"Explain what I've just said to your neighbor"—throughout the learning experience.

5. Expect Variance

Put two people in the same room and ask them to watch an excerpt from a film. Five minutes after the film has ended, ask them what it was about. Five weeks later do the same thing. Five months later repeat the process. Not only will you find a difference between the two individuals' perceptions, but also over time there will be a difference in how each individual remembers. Memory is more about reconstitution than recall. What we remember varies by individual and will distort over time. Space your review sessions to keep content recall high. Actively involve students in reviewing with each other. Have them explain Mind Maps to each other, swap notes, and question each other on their own notes.

6. Use a Variety of Testing Procedures to Improve Recall

The one strategy that, more than any other, will help a learner recall information needed for an exam is self-testing. Yet most students run in fear of the self-test. Teach students how to test themselves and each other and encourage them to do so. An example is hiding a page and trying to remember what is on it. Test informally, frequently, and with variety. Make sure that you debrief both the emotional and the academic dimensions of the test experience. Doing so helps students who believe they are the only ones who have an erratic memory in test situations to understand the anxiety dimension of tests.

7. Use Places, Faces, and Spaces

We naturally remember locations, faces, and physical positions. We are good at doing so and would not have survived as a species if we were not. Use lots of places, faces, and spaces in classroom examples. When you use learning posters, make their content, their appearance, and their spatial position part of the learning: What did it tell us? Can you remember what it looked like? Where was it and why?

Memory Models

The best memory techniques involve multiple systems.

Outlined in this section are some simple mnemonics for memory techniques. The first—IFR—derives from early Greek writings and reminds us that, should we wish to improve memory performance, doing so requires a conscious decision. The second—SPECS—provides you and your students with the five simplest memory tools.

Commit to IFR

IFR stands for

Intent. You have to want to remember the information. A purpose and a personal value are important.

File. You need multiple systems—such as any combination of the five described below—for effective remembering.

Rehearse. You need to go over the information a few times; a little at a time and often is best. Spaced testing also helps.

Use Your Memory **SPECS**

SPECS stands for

See it. People are very good at visual and spatial recall.

Personalize it. People remember information with personal significance.

Exaggerate it. The unusual, out of place, or distinctive gets remembered.

Connect it. Links to other known information provide quick associations.

Share it. Summarizing or teaching something to others makes it memorable.

Let's take an example. The class is going to learn about mean, median, and mode in math. To help they are going to construct a living graph using students from six different grades. You have arranged for four students—two boys and two girls—from each grade to be temporarily released from class to help. First, the class arranges the students in a long line in order of shoe size and notes who is where. Then they organize them along a horizontal axis. Each student has to stand behind the shoe size that matches his or her own. Record how many students wear each shoe size. This activity generates lots of questions about sample size, the difference between boys and girls, and so on. Finally, the class constructs a visual reminder of the shape of the graph using a long rope. With curtain rods or yardsticks, subdivide the graph to represent its various features.

This example involves several memory-enhancing features:

- Students see what is going on.

- The information is personalized and students are actively involved in creating it.

- The information is exaggerated because graphs do not usually involve humans.

- It is connected because it provokes questions and comparisons.

- Because they will have to explain it to others—and perhaps position themselves on the graph to illustrate mean, median, and mode or to talk about sample size—the experience is also shared.

Chapter 4 ————————————————————

Accelerated Learning: Advice and Guidance

In Chapter 4 You Will Find

- ▶ Homework
- ▶ Effective Note-Taking
- ▶ Smart Grading
- ▶ Great Ways to Make Grading Smarter
- ▶ Great Lesson Openers
- ▶ Great Classroom Motivators
- ▶ Great Ways to Get into Groups
- ▶ How to Get Quiet
- ▶ How to Use Physical Breaks
- ▶ Great Ways to Use Music
- ▶ Watch Your Language
- ▶ Visual Display
- ▶ Using Technology
- ▶ Using Communication Technology to Support Accelerated Learning
- ▶ Designing Accelerated Learning Web Pages
- ▶ Examples of Accelerated Learning Lesson Plans
- ▶ Your Questions Answered
- ▶ Introducing Accelerated Learning into Your School

Homework

People who work sitting down get paid more than people who work standing up.
—Ogden Nash

The assignment of homework causes controversy and, for some teachers and students alike, no small amount of heartache. Why do we do it? Some researchers argue that homework disrupts families, overburdens children, and limits learning. Others suggest that time spent on homework can be correlated to achievement at the secondary level, particularly among older students. Eleventh- and twelfth-grade British students who spent seven or more hours per week on subject homework achieved, on average, a third of a grade higher than those of similar ability and gender who spent fewer than two hours a week on homework. The evidence on homework and achievement for primary-age students is slim. The "for" and "against" homework camps line up their arguments as follows:

The "for" camp argue that

- findings consistently show that at the secondary level time spent on homework correlates to improved grades.
- homework is a link to parents and encourages parental involvement.
- many schools have homework policies and strategies in place.
- it helps learners develop independent learning and learning-to-learn skills.
- parents are generally in favor of homework assignments, even though they may have concerns about the amount of time it takes.
- parents become involved in three ways: encouraging children to do the homework, removing distractions so it can be done and, with younger children, providing direct assistance.
- students who spend more time on homework have more positive attitudes toward school (however, social, class, and gender variables have yet to be properly factored into this finding).
- the best type of homework encourages self-reliance without "making it harder."

The "against" camp argue that

- homework can disrupt family life and cause friction in relationships.

- research on the value of homework is, at the very best, uneven.

- homework is assigned to conform to external pressures rather than for sound learning outcomes.

- it is biased in favor of advantaged homes.

- most homework involves rote, repetition, or drill and has negative effects on attitude.

- it can reinforce bad learning habits.

- it increases teachers' workload.

- in some instances, it is so ineptly done it is counterproductive and causes classroom conflict.

- one in five parents believes that the school's homework practice is inconsistent.

- direct parental involvement in helping with homework does not raise achievement; achievement is a function of the type of assistance given which, again, disadvantages poorly educated parents.

Is there a way to make homework effective? Imaginative solutions such as homework clubs, drop-in study centers, and designated spaces in public libraries have all been tried with some success. Providing a safe, regulated, warm, and inviting space seems to lure in a wider community of learners for after-school sessions. Voluntary sessions often have a seductive power, and many schools indicate surprise at how readily difficult students get involved.

In schools where homework is planned by a team well in advance and is seen as an integral part of extending the lesson, the situation is better. Some schools have banned certain types of homework—such as copying, coloring, finishing off, doing ten more—with some success. Such schools actively promote extension, or "thinking," homework. Others plan that given units will not be taught in class but tutored and, as such, will be homework units with supported self-study resources. Teachers using this approach need to plan well in advance but benefit from freed-up teaching time. Here are ideas for increasing the value of homework.

1. Choice

Allow students some choice in how they present their homework; for example, using a concept map, flow chart, diagram, cartoon, poem, book review, and so on. This flexibility will appeal to different learning styles.

2. Transform

Taking information presented in one form and presenting it in another is great for reinforcement, For example, have students transform text into a Mind Map, concept map, storyboard, or graph, or vice versa.

3. Reduce

Have students reduce the information to its essentials. For example, reduce the lesson to three key points and be prepared to justify your choice, or identify the key character/scene/cause and why you rejected the other possibilities.

4. Prepare

For example, prepare a booklet of self-contained homework assignments for the unit being studied. Incorporate a number of "milestone" lessons to check on progress.

5. Cut Up

Cut the exercises out of old textbooks, or download exercises from a website. Paste these exercises on cards and laminate them for durability.

6. Decision Making

Give students an envelope containing statements of fact and ideas. Ask students to distinguish between the two and place the items in rank order according to criteria; for example, why did the United States lose the war in Vietnam?

7. Quiz

Ask students to prepare questions on the topic for use in the next lesson, following the format of a popular TV quiz game; for example, Who Wants to be a Millionaire, where questions will range from the very easy ($5.00) to very hard ($500,000, $1 million).

8. Model Answers

Give students the opportunity to grade a model answer.

9. Ranking

Rank pieces of work according to well-understood and previously discussed assessment criteria.

10. Mistakes

There is no activity more popular than spotting the deliberate mistakes in a diagram or piece of text.

11. Pyramid, or 3, 2, 1 Block Review

On sticky notes or in squares drawn on a sheet of paper, students write

> one thing I already know,
> two questions I still want to ask, and
> the three most important things I have learned.

Assign this or another review technique for homework before a Consolidation phase classroom activity (see page 37).

Effective Note-Taking

Keep a diary and one day it will keep you.
—Mae West

How about making note-taking more interactive and allowing students to record information in a way that aligns with the learning cycle? Interactive student notebooks reach students with a wide range of learning styles, allow for a unique personal response, and give students the freedom and creativity to express themselves in a variety of ways; for example, Venn diagrams to show relationships, cartoons, Mind Maps.

Here is how such note-taking can work. The notebook is divided into left and right sides, the left side for student exploration and the right side for class notes and other teacher-driven content.

LEFT SIDE	RIGHT SIDE
Students process new ideas	**Teacher gives input**
Students work out an understanding of new material in a personal way; for example, using illustrations, diagrams, poetry, color, graphics, concept maps.	Class notes
Students express their opinions and record their feelings/reactions.	"Must-know" information
Students can pose themselves key questions.	Handouts
Students can review/preview.	Discussion notes
Students can explore new ideas.	
STUDENT OWNS!	**TEACHER OWNS!**

This system encourages students to become engaged in learning and to actively process information. They are doing something with the new ideas, often using their preferred learning style, and really enjoying being given the opportunity to express their own opinions about what they are learning. It does not have to be boring for the teacher either! Imitation is one of the most important ways we learn, so model how to think and organize information for your right-hand side of the notebook.

Another example more finely tuned to the learning cycle works as follows. A notebook can be divided into sections that reflect the various elements of the cycle; for example, a "connect" section and a "reviewing our learning" section. The center section of the book can be reserved for recording information and for learning activities. The following is an example using a humanities unit on conflict and cooperation.

Connect Section

In the first lesson students are given the key questions that will be addressed within the topic. For example,

- What are the causes of local conflict?
- What are the causes of international conflict?
- How are local conflicts resolved?

Students take a two-page spread and create a "big picture" that includes the topic title, key questions, and a series of images, cartoons, diagrams, and so on that will help them remember the main ideas. As they progress through the topic, they can regularly return to the "big picture" spread and add further information and images.

The connect section can be used at the start of each class to connect the upcoming lesson to the previously presented information. Students could also from time to time use it as a review page at the end of a lesson by adding new ideas and information dealt with in that lesson.

Activate Section

This section will be used for the major activity of the lesson. This section of the book could contain appropriate maps, notes, time lines, and decisions that students have worked to compile. Cross-references to the connect page can be made as appropriate.

In the example of the study of local conflict, students may continue, after looking at an introductory video, by considering case studies of local conflicts and identifying other causes of conflict before discovering the mechanisms available for the resolution of these conflicts. In the activate section of their notebooks, students record their findings using the method of their choice.

Demonstrate Section

This section gives students the opportunity to explain their new understanding in relation to the topic using strategies such as Beat the Examiner or a simulated press conference resulting in a front-page scoop. These are useful techniques if you wish your students to record and retain a body of notes for later review. (These and other ideas are explored in more depth in "Demonstration Phase Activities," pages 33–36.)

Reviewing Our Learning Section

At the end of a lesson students may be asked, for example, to write down five things they have learned that they did not know at the start of the lesson. Here students can draw and complete their block reviews. They can also review the processes they have been through and reflect on how well these have worked. Any review activity you choose can be accommodated here. As they collect the various review methods in this section, students will quickly become familiar with the different ways of reviewing their work.

Smart Grading

Learning is formed more by feedback than by instruction.

In 1998 Professors Black and Wiliam (King's College, London) published an article detailing their findings from a research project entitled "Inside the Black Box." The project focused on the impact of various assessment strategies on raising student achievement. They found that where assessment was used formatively, there were significant improvements in achievement.

The research described in *Assessment for Learning: Beyond the Black Box* (Assessment Reform Group 1999) concluded that improving learning through assessment depends on the following five key factors:

- the provision of effective feedback to students
- the active involvement of students in their own learning
- the adjustment of teaching to take into account the results of assessment
- a recognition of the profound influence assessment has on the motivation and self-esteem of students
- the need for students to be able to assess themselves and understand how to improve

Here are some ideas about how Assessment for Learning principles can underpin, support, and enhance each stage of the Accelerated Learning Cycle.

Connection Phase

At the heart of Assessment for Learning is the sharing of clear and concise learning intentions.
—Shirley Clarke

The starting point for effective lesson planning is the consideration of learning goals. What do I want students to know or be able to do at the end of fifty minutes with me that they could not do before?

Agree on the learning goals with students, write them on a large piece of chart paper, and pin them up somewhere prominent in the classroom. Actively involve students in the construction of the learning goals. Refer to them throughout the lesson.

Even better, engage students in extended dialogue about learning goals. For example, arrange a rope on the floor. Identify one end as "a lot," and the other as "nothing." Ask the students what they know about the topic (for example, "What do you know about George Washington?"). Students stand at the point on the rope that represents their current knowledge. Then you ask about their level of interest in the topic (for example, "What do you want to know about George Washington?") and again students arrange themselves on the rope. A variation used by Paul Ginnis (2005) is to make a cross on the floor using masking tape and have one axis represent prior knowledge and the other level of interest (see "The Axis of Learning," page 26).

You can then arrange groups to include enthusiasts with skeptics, and the uninformed with the knowledgeable. The new groups generate lots and lots of questions. The questions are then categorized to form broad learning goals.

Two other strategies are WILF and TIBS. WILF, symbolized by a goldfish, stands for *What I'm Looking For,* in which you make clear what your expectations are. Alternatively, for greater student involvement, the goldfish could be called WALT, for *What Are We Learning Today?* TIBS is a large cat and stands for *This Is Because,* in which you try to make the learning relevant to the learners. Students can be greeted by these characters every lesson.

Assessment for Learning is also about training students to be quality assessors and to recognize what constitutes a good piece of work. In the Connection phase you might also engage students in a discussion about how they will know they have been successful. Success criteria should also be agreed on and displayed. Look at the following example from a learning-to-learn lesson:

What I'm Looking For is for you to practice your concept mapping skills by creating a unique concept map of the information I have given you.

This Is Because concept mapping is an important technique that will help you to make sense of a large amount of information very quickly.

How will we know we have been successful? You collaboratively establish with students that a quality concept map would be colorful and contain both key vocabulary and images. It would clearly show links between topics or ideas. These would be summarized and posted in the classroom. You might even show some concept maps that students created the year before, asking students to rank them in order of quality or to select which one they think is best and to explain their choice.

Activation Phase

Most teachers answer their own questions.

Use open-ended questioning techniques throughout the lesson to get students to think about their work in relation to the success criteria. Allow thinking time. Research has shown that most teachers answer their own questions and allow an average of between 0.7 and 1.3 seconds for thinking time. Teachers also rarely plan the questions they will ask during a lesson. Encourage students to ask questions of each other and to pair up and share possible answers.

Use grouping effectively and flexibly. Facilitate peer tutoring by placing students who demonstrate a good understanding of the topic with those who do not.

Demonstration Phase

Show what you know.

What better way to demonstrate understanding of a topic than to create a test for it? Students can work in pairs to identify what they think should be on the test and to generate test items and responses. They can then give the tests to their friends, score them, and provide feedback.

Make sure students are asked to demonstrate understanding only in relation to the established success criteria. For example, if the learning goal of the lesson was, "By the end of this lesson, you will be able to give three examples of sedimentary rocks," it would be unfair to expect students to be able to give a full description of how metamorphic rocks are formed.

Consolidation Phase

Allow time for feedback and reflection.

This phase is where students can really get involved in feedback. Students could assess each other's presentations and suggest ways in which they could be improved. It is, of course, important to teach students how to give feedback sensitively and appropriately. Feedback must relate only to the success criteria. Use a feedback sheet or a scoring template to guide student feedback. Ask them to concentrate on only one aspect of a presentation at first and gradually expand their efforts as they get better at assessment and feedback.

This phase also offers an important opportunity for students to reflect on their own work and to make judgments about its quality, perhaps setting themselves targets for improvement. Self-assessment sheets or learning diaries are useful tools for this purpose. Make sure everyone views self-assessment as a thinking and talking activity, not just as a writing one.

Great Ways to Make Grading Smarter

The single most powerful modification that enhances achievement is feedback. The simplest prescription for improving education must be "dollops of feedback."
—J. A. Hattie

The research reported here shows conclusively that formative assessment does improve learning. The gains in achievement appear to be quite considerable . . . amongst the largest ever noted for educational interventions.
—Paul Black and Dylan Wiliam

The more involved the learner is, the better.

The less work the teacher does, the better.

The nearer to the real experience the feedback is, the better.

The more specific the feedback, the better.

The clearer and more readily understood the assessment criteria, the better.

Our first recommendation is that you remove the word *grading* from the school vocabulary. Do so immediately! Inform parents that the school wants to involve learners more so you will be creating more opportunities for improvement through feedback.

In research done by Robert Marzano (2001), teachers who had the greatest increase in raising achievement were those who helped students to understand through comparison and classification activities. Try to weave into your feedback strategy lots of opportunities for making comparisons, ordering, and providing classification systems.

Criteria first

Record the criteria for assessment at the top of a piece of work before students start on it.

Join the dots

Identify mistakes with a green dot and no more. The student then makes the correction.

Bulleted suggestions for improvement

Give no more than three very specific bulleted suggestions for improvement. The student records them in a notebook and over time they form the focus for learning review.

Peer grading

Using a rubber stamp or reproducible feedback form, a peer from within an ability group gives a piece of work a preliminary evaluation, marking four positive features for each feature needing improvement.

Trial grading

Photocopy sample assignments and have small groups evaluate them against the criteria you describe. They assign each sample a grade and justify their decisions.

Grading in moderation

Students grade the samples as above, then place them in rank order according to quality.

Critical friends

In pairs and working from a set of prompt questions, students ask questions that require the creator of the work to explain what he or she has done and why. Nothing is written down at this stage, and the creator has the opportunity to redraft the work before receiving a grade.

Hunt for evidence

Provide criteria for success and, in pairs or threes, students search sample assignments for evidence that they are present. In this and in other activities like it, the imperative is to find evidence of successes not failures.

Agree on the criteria

Assessment criteria are shared, discussed, then rewritten in student-friendly language and presented in a visual display as a reminder.

E-easy way

Groups of students share their draft essays via e-mail. They work in small networked learning communities! Each member of the community is given a different task so that there is little chance of duplication.

Rolling audit

Rather than grading every piece of written work, audit the assignments and grade only every third piece. Have students on a rotating grading regime so that for each assignment, you grade one-third of the students' papers. Those who are on "grading hold" work with others in peer-review teams and self-assess by evaluating their work against the comments you made on other work. This ensures formative dialogue about work while preventing you from burning out.

Taxonomy of errors

Give examples of different categories of errors and discuss them at length as a class so that grading becomes a question of identifying the category of error various students made. This information can then be used to provide group tutoring in common problem areas.

Tablet PCs

Use tablet PCs with wireless links to record formative assessment of students as you interact with them in lessons. This information can then be downloaded and saved for later use—perhaps sent to an individual student's e-mail address or made available via password on the school's website.

Pre-drafting

Before submitting essays or written work, students share them in pairs or supportive small groups and promptly correct any errors or problems revealed thereby.

Give time

In lessons give time for students to respond to written feedback.

Prompts

Help students to improve work with scaffolded prompts, fill-in-the-blank statements, or examples.

Great Lesson Openers

Engage attention in order to direct it.

Adapt these ideas for lessons or for training days. Humor and movement will help capture students' interest.

Question/answer cards. Each student receives a card with a question on one side and an unrelated answer on the reverse. Students have to find the answer to their question, which is on the reverse of another's question card.

Blockhead teacher. Get the class to help you with an obvious problem you "can't figure out."

Hunt for autographs. Prepare a list of attributes and skills. Students match these up with classmates who have those characteristics and get their autographs.

Time limited brainstorming. Students (as individuals, as pairs, or in groups) race against the clock to brainstorm everything they know about a new topic.

Three-minute summary. One student from each group takes exactly three minutes to summarize information for the others.

Press conference. In groups, students present their information from the three-minute session in summary form. Questions from the floor follow. The event is run along the lines of a press conference.

Sticky note parade. Each pair writes one fact or statement about a topic on a sticky note. The sticky notes are placed on the board. The class then looks at the notes and classifies them by repositioning them on the board.

Milling around. The class mills around and, on cue, students introduce themselves to someone and describe in thirty seconds one thing they have learned so far. On cue they swap roles for thirty seconds. Then a new round begins.

Up in the elevator. Pairs of students pretend to be in an elevator traveling between the first and tenth floors. In the ninety seconds between the first and the tenth floors, they have to find out what the other student has been learning that day.

Feely bag. Place in a bag five items that relate to the current lesson. One student reaches into the bag and describes an item by feel. The others discuss what the object might be and how it relates to the topic.

Artifact challenge. Use artifacts or props to prompt questions and discussion.

Arouse curiosity! At the start of a topic, show an object or objects and ask students to guess their use. The same principle can apply to photographs by asking students what they think is happening.

Intriguing issues! Turn the topic into an intriguing issue. Instead of the usual rather flat and dry introduction to a topic: "Today we are going to study the water cycle," try, "Today we will ask the question, How can we ensure that everybody on the planet has access to fresh water?"

Give personal meaning. Have students describe a scenario related to the current topic. For example, "Imagine you have woken up today in a world without electricity. Spend ten minutes writing an account of the next hour of your day."

Involve. Show a carefully chosen, powerful visual image (in a slide or photograph). Ask students to describe everything they see, then invite some students to "step into" the slide or photograph and act out what they think is happening. You can pretend to have a microphone and interview the students using well-directed questions. The visual image should be clearly tied to your learning objectives; illustrate key events, issues, or concepts; be something students can act out; and be fun or unusual.

The ambassador's reception. The scene is a sophisticated ambassador's reception. Classical music plays; students circulate, chatting to each other about the highlights from the previous lesson. They carry appointment cards on which are written four deliberately provocative statements related to the topic about to be studied. On the flip side of the card is a picture of a clock with spaces to write in appointments at 3 o'clock, 6 o'clock, 9 o'clock, and 12 o'clock. When the music stops, students turn to the person nearest to them and discuss the first statement. Allow them a few minutes to do this, then warn them that the music is about to start again. At this point, students write each other's names in the 3 o'clock appointment slot and agree to see each other later. The music starts and students once again move off into the social swirl. Stop the music again a little while later and students repeat the exercise, this time discussing the second statement before making a 6 o'clock appointment. This continues until each student has discussed four statements and made four appointments that he or she will keep later in the lesson or at some future time. Each of the statements discussed has stimulated thought about the learning to come and you have cleverly set up four different pairings for pair/share work later in the lesson.

Humor. Using an overhead projector, display a cartoon in some way connected to the topic. The Internet is a great source for these.

Let there be music. Choose a suitable and contextualizing piece of music or song either to create the mood or to provide a context for the learning to come. Using irony can be effective; for example, playing "Another Day in Paradise" by Phil Collins at the beginning of a module on homelessness or Blondie's "Atomic" at the beginning of a lesson on the structure of the atom.

Overhead projector silhouette. Place an object related to the upcoming lesson on an overhead projector so that students can see only the silhouette. Ask students in pairs to guess what the object is and what it may have to do with the lesson.

Arrive on, or ahead of, time!

Great Classroom Motivators

Motivation is emotion in motion.

Sell the benefits. Explain what we all gain from the outcomes of the learning. What makes us better off as a result of doing this?

Share the process. Explain the methodology for learning.

Show your interest. The basic unit of motivational currency is the interest of another human—being esteemed by an influencer.

Give constructive feedback. Give specific bulleted suggestions for improvement that students can act on immediately.

Praise discreetly. Praise that is private and personal, not public and paraded, is the best for many—especially boys.

Use proximity modeling. Do not pretend everyone can be perfect like a celebrity star if they try hard enough. Some might be able to shape up a bit and take it from there.

Chunk the challenges. A little challenge, presented often, is the best way to improve. Ask yourself what 1 percent improvement steps are possible for the task at hand. Identify those 1 percent steps.

Practice little acts of kindness. Give something of value away to the most difficult student and expect nothing in return. A copy of *Field and Stream* may be enough to change your relationship with the hostile boy who loves fishing.

Rely on the security of a ritual. In threatening situations, a ritual makes people feel safe. In high-challenge situations, ritualized, shared moments help people cope.

Use two-dimensional debriefing. Debrief students about their knowledge and feelings after tests and mock exams. This lets students know that everyone gets stressed in an exam. And, besides, they are more interested in the feelings dimension.

Provide meaningful choice in lessons.

At the end of the day, students will engage in a lesson if

- the topic is intrinsically interesting.
- the topic is relevant—students can see some purpose to learning about it.
- they can make a connection (or connections) to prior learning or their own lives.
- the students like you—it is important to take time to build good relationships.

Great Ways to Get into Groups

Learning is a social activity enhanced by shared inquiry.

Group work protocols throughout the school. Agree on and put into your staff handbook protocols for group work that every teacher can readily use. Doing so makes grouping easier for students and staff alike.

Group work protocol for your classroom. Agree on simple protocols for moving into and between groups and display these prominently.

Home and away groups. Home groups are friendship groups in which members have high levels of familiarity. Away groups are non-friendship groups with lower levels of familiarity. Have students move back and forth between the two during projects.

Group roles. Assign roles to group members and have laminated cards that outline what students do in each nominated role.

Groupings by purpose.

Random selection.

Mixed ability grouping.

Press corps. This group's job is to report on the activities and progress of other groups. A press conference of findings can follow.

Envoys. Each group sends an envoy to each of the other groups to share findings or to share or gather information.

Building Up and Scaling Down. Students begin a task in pairs, then regroup into groups of four, then of eight.

Suggested Group Roles

The coordinator is responsible for making sure everyone in the group understands the task at hand, is involved in decision making, and takes on a role in the generation of solutions or outcomes.

The scribe is responsible for recording decisions made.

The clock watcher is responsible for ensuring that the activity and its component stages are completed within established time limits.

The collector is responsible for obtaining any resources that will be needed.

The checker is responsible for ensuring that what is planned actually occurs.

The communicator is responsible for talking to other groups and for summarizing findings.

Good Questions for Group Members to Ask

○ What do we need to do?

○ Where should we go to obtain help?

○ When must we have it done?

○ Who needs to do what?

○ How will we know we've done a good job?

○ What methods are best?

○ What will we have learned by doing this?

How to Get Quiet

I will not yell "she's dead" during roll call.
I will not sleep through my education.
I will not grease the wall bars.
I will not dissect things without instructions.
—Bart's blackboard lines, "The Simpsons"

1. Carpet the classroom.

2. Teach appropriate sound levels for learning as a whole-class activity and practice them.

3. Teach good listening skills.

4. Avoid viewing silence as necessarily purposeful and always conducive to learning.

5. Provide lots of opportunities for structured paired and small-group discussion.

6. Lower your voice.

7. Ensure all new furniture has rubber-tipped feet! Buy blinds that roll rather than pull vertically.

8. Replace chalkboards with whiteboards.

9. Use a noise meter visual to show what sort of volume level is appropriate for any given activity.

10. Play quiet, restful background music and gradually lower the volume.

11. Play natural sounds, such as birdsong, quietly in the background.

12. Practice extended visualization as part of classroom learning.

13. Review lesson content using a passive concert: Students close their eyes, rest their heads, and listen as you review the key material to the accompaniment of quiet background music.

14. Give the very young fidgets noiseless items to fiddle with, so that they do not distract everyone else.

15. Agree with the class on the criteria for a top-quality audience. Post these on the classroom wall and thereafter signal your request for a quality audience by saying, "Can I have a quality audience in five seconds, please? 5, 4, 3, 2, 1. Quality audience now, please." Hold your hand in the air as a physical cue. Be persistent; this is important.

16. Use your position in class. For example, always stand at the same place in the classroom when asking for quiet. Pretty soon, your class will start to associate your moving to this particular spot with a signal for quiet.

17. Establish important classroom rituals. For example, we always start lessons by reviewing what we learned from last time. When someone else is talking, everyone puts down their pens and listens.

How to Use Physical Breaks

Stasis fatigue: the state of being immobilized for too long.

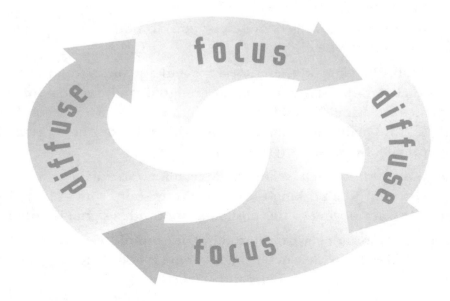

1. Recognize that no one is good at sitting still for extended periods. Do not expect the class to be able to sit with focused attention for long periods.

2. Try to make diffusion a part of the lesson. An example would be a short, timed review where students cross the room and describe to others three things they have already learned.

3. Adopt a focus–diffuse–focus–diffuse model, in which periods of sustained attention are separated with short structured breaks.

4. As a crude rule of thumb (with no basis in science!), use chronological age plus one as a maxim: With ten-year-olds, work for eleven or twelve minutes before a diffusion activity.

5. Practice stretching exercises regularly.

6. Use modeling and physical learning—number lines, continuity lines, body sculptures, living graphs—as integral parts of your lesson.

7. Familiarize yourself with brain-break activities and their different applications.

8. Practice classroom yoga, deep breathing, and relaxation techniques with your class; incorporate these strategies into mental rehearsals of learning.

9. Plan at least two short breaks for every hour of classroom teaching.

10. Stay physically fit yourself.

Great Ways to Use Music

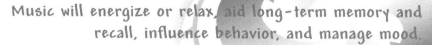

Music will energize or relax, aid long-term memory and recall, influence behavior, and manage mood.

1. Use music only in ways that aid learning, and be clear in your own mind how using music in your classroom aids learning.

2. Choose the music yourself and have only one source of music—students may not bring in their own music or players.

3. Categorize the music by learning purpose: energizing, relaxing, focusing, themed, timed task, and visualization.

4. Discuss how and why music is used to aid learning; find out who enjoys learning to music and who finds it distracting.

5. Use calming music at the beginning of lessons.

6. Rewrite the lyrics of familiar songs to incorporate key content.

7. Rewrite lyrics as a whole-class activity, starting with key vocabulary.

8. Take familiar songs and replace some of the words with your own key vocabulary.

9. Use music to signify celebratory or ritual events, such as an end-of-unit quiz.

10. Play music as students get ready to take tests and exams to provide a sense of familiarity and promote relaxation.

11. Use music to create a mood; for example, play "Eye of the Tiger" from the film *Rocky* for challenge.

12. Use music as a timing device; for example, play the theme from *Mission Impossible* while clearing up.

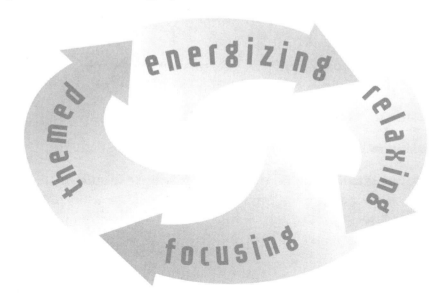

Watch Your Language

The language that is used in the classroom plays a part in shaping the experience of speaker and listener. Here are a few suggestions for monitoring your classroom talk.

Avoid teacherese. Phrases such as "woe betide" are never heard except in a classroom! Adding to the confusion is teachers' occasional tendency to indulge in ambiguities: "What do we not do when we go to the assembly?" "Can we take off our coats now, please?" Evidence shows that students' confusion about the teacher's meaning can contribute to misbehavior.

Avoid too much "yes, but" thinking. If you are predisposed to find fault, it will be reflected in your choice of words. "I agree with you, however . . ." has a very different effect than "I agree with you and. . . ."

Use choice drivers. Choose to say, "George, what will you do with your Gameboy? Switch it off and put it away, or give it to me to look after for you?" rather than "Put it away or else!"

Avoid superfluous questions. "Now, do you all understand?" "Has everyone finished yet?" "How is everyone getting on?" These are not very useful and amount to mere noise.

Experiment with language sandwiches. Sandwich positive and negative statements in different combinations to see which work best for you. For example, a positive-negative-positive sandwich is "We are making good progress. I notice that you have not yet completed the exercise. I'm confident you'll succeed before the end of the lesson."

Use the word *learning* more often. "Let's get on with our learning" is more attractive and more useful than "Let's get on with our work."

Avoid overusing the word *grading*. Replace it with the word *feedback*.

Avoid overusing the word *ability*. Replace it with the word *abilities*.

Use "noticing" language. You describe in objective terms a student's (or students') learning behavior. For example, "I noticed that when I introduced this topic there were lots of good questions, which included. . . ." You can then invite thoughts as to why what you noticed was noteworthy.

Use "earshotting." This simple technique involves deliberately letting people hear you make positive comments about them. You make the remarks to someone else within earshot, knowing that even if what you say is not overheard, it will be passed on.

Use future focus not past prejudice. The fact that a student misbehaved in a given way yesterday should not be a reason to hold his or her behavior for ransom today. To effect positive changes in behavior, choose to use the language of possibility: "What would it be like if?" "How might you do this differently?" "When you've perfected it, what will it be like?"

Match predicates. This is a neurolinguistic processing technique that involves matching the listener's language preference to improve rapport. A preference for visual processing is often reflected in the use of visual predicates. ("I see what you mean." "It looks good to me."). Auditory processing is sounded out in the use of auditory predicates. ("I hear what you're saying."' "It sounded alarm bells for me.") Kinesthetic processing is often reflected in the use of physical predicates. ("It feels fine." "It moved me.") When talking with students, listen carefully to the words they use and adjust your language to use similar terms.

Say what you want, rather than what you don't want. Saying what you want makes everyday dialogue easier. For example, if you have specified what good listening behavior is like, you can catch it more easily when students display it.

Visual Display

The brain is first an image processor before it is a word processor.

Learning posters. Create very large, easy-to-read posters that summarize the essential learning points and post them on your classroom wall. Laminate the posters so that they can be reused. Test students' recall of the posters. Have them copy the poster in their notebooks and practice mentally rehearsing the look of the poster. Move the laminated learning posters and the related words (see below) into the hallway.

Related vocabulary arranged in families. Surround the learning poster with related vocabulary. Never place key vocabulary in rows. Try to link the key vocabulary to the content of the learning poster through their physical placement. Use the connecting words to develop understanding of key concepts.

Learning behaviors. Use cryptic descriptors of useful learning behaviors. For example, "Getting stuck is not a problem, staying stuck is. Good learners practice getting unstuck." These can be related to themes, form the topic for class lessons, or appear on the school website, on screen savers, and in parent newsletters.

Poster rehearsals. Use the learning posters and their families of related key vocabulary as core tools when reviewing for tests.

Interactive displays. If students' work is to be displayed, make the display significant by drawing attention to it. Position the work in public places. Make the display interactive so that close scrutiny is required and rewarded. Do not display work through force of habit, for wallpaper, or for any purpose other than one that supports learning.

Passports to success. Display success criteria prominently in a classroom poster. Give students laminated, playing-card-size versions of the criteria poster and use them as classroom prompt cards. These cards can be used as the basis of classroom activities.

Audiovisual aids. Make the most of audiovisual aids. Use them as you would any other significant learning resource. Optimize student access and use.

Steps to success. Prominently display the steps necessary to improve performance in given activities, say, creative writing. Reinforce them by having students record their own versions in their notebooks.

Using an overhead projector. Use color on your transparencies. Prepare them beforehand so that you can incorporate images. Encourage students to get used to using the overhead projector for simple and effective summaries of group findings, information that has been learned, and points of view. Visual prompts make it easier for all students to talk through their findings in a coherent way. Be creative! An English teacher made a silhouette for a session on Shakespearean sonnets by placing a single rose on an overhead projector. She then introduced the topic against this backdrop; the effect was quite mesmerizing. (You could have students guess what the objects silhouetted on the overhead projector are as a way of hooking them into a topic.)

Thinking wall. Build up a "thinking" culture in your classroom by having a large display of Bloom's (1956) taxonomy on one wall with associated thinking vocabulary for each level of thinking (page 22). For example, for knowledge, the lowest level on the thinking ladder, you could display words such as *repeat* and *recall*. Throughout lessons students could be asked to indicate what level of thinking is taking place.

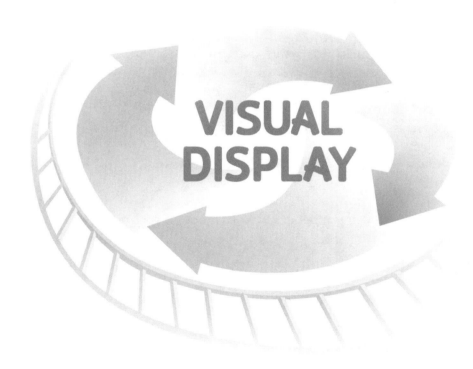

Using Technology

The technology tail should not wag the learning dog.

A structured model for engaging learning becomes even more important when there is a proliferation of information technologies in and around classrooms. Here are some considerations:

Is it the right tool for the job? There is no "right" technology. It is simply right for a particular purpose at a particular moment in time. At one stage, the two-color mimeograph machine was the height of resource sophistication.

Impress me! Expensive technology brings pressure on staff to quickly show expertise in its use. Prepare for this by scheduling a training session before installation. Do not delegate the training to the suppliers!

Beware nerd creep. Love of technology for its own sake exerts a negative pressure on good teaching and squeezes it out.

Ability diverges. Disparities in staff use and understanding of the classroom applications of new technology will quickly widen.

Change looms! Remember when the now-obsolete eight-track tapes were the future of recording? Do not put all your investment into one type of technology.

Curriculum lags behind technology. The curriculum is not rethought as quickly as the technology is.

Fit the technology to the purpose. Use a balance of technology that is a good fit for your purposes rather than putting all your eggs in one expensive basket.

Look out for Fifi: Fit it, forget it! Avoid investing in expensive technology and then forgetting about it. Review its use and influence regularly.

Don't pile up expectations. Avoid piling new learning and teaching demands on top of the existing model of what is needed.

Figure the total cost of ownership. Factor in training costs—time and personnel—when devising your technology strategy.

Think loopy. Think of class work, private study, and homework as a loop system.

Mind the gap. Use technology to decrease the gaps between home and school, community and school, and the world and school.

Whose is the technology? Consider how the technology actively and meaningfully engages learners; investigate its use by structured classroom observation. Ask who uses it and when. How does it influence classroom interactions? What happens to problem solving? Discussion? How does individualization exhibit itself?

Plan for the novelty wearing off.

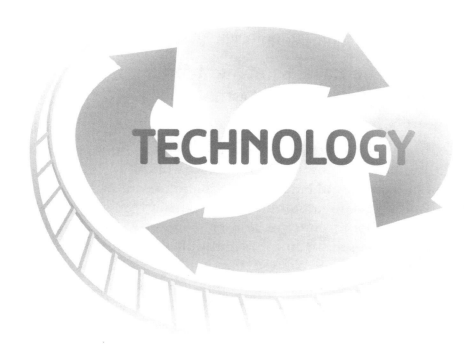

Using Communication Technology to Support Accelerated Learning

It is not the amount of RAM you have that is important but how you use your equipment.

Communication technology is not just about computers but any piece of technology that supports or enables communication, from cell phones to DVD players, from overhead projectors to tape recorders. You do not have to have the latest and most expensive equipment or the greatest number of megapixels to use communication technology effectively in the classroom.

Getting Started: The Basic Equipment for the Twenty-First-Century Classroom

Ideally every learning space would have the following:

- At least one personal computer with a link to the Internet (World Wide Web) or to the school intranet (internal network).
- A pair of speakers so you have access to sound. We are always amazed at how many people forget about sound. Speakers are fairly inexpensive, about $25.
- A microphone that fits into the personal computer. A microphone allows you or your students to create sound files and use brilliant pieces of software like Camtasia Studio (see page 75).
- A inexpensive digital camera. The ones that are most useful in the classroom are the most basic ones with a port to download to a computer. Do not play the "megapixels" game and buy a fancy camera that comes with its own software.
- Access to a printer. This does not mean every room has to have a printer, but reasonable access is important. Get a robust black-and-white printer for regular use. Color does make a huge difference and the printers themselves are not expensive, but the replacement ink cartridges are.
- An electronic whiteboard or portable data projector. If your budget runs to it, then an electronic whiteboard or a portable data projector makes a big difference in the classroom and opens up a whole range of possibilities. If your budget does not extend that far, then buy a lead that connects your computer to a television screen. This is a much cheaper alternative that allows you to display what is on the computer screen to the whole class.

TECHNOLOGY

Six Must-Have Pieces of Software

Inspiration (or for younger students Kidspiration). This software allows the user to combine key vocabulary and images to create "concept," or thinking, maps.

Camtasia Studio. This software video records the computer screen as you work on it and records your voice as you explain what you are doing.

PowerPoint. If used effectively, this excellent piece of presentation software can be highly visual and engaging. It is a good tool for supporting student presentations, enabling them to talk through and explain their work and ideas.

Hot Potatoes. Available for free download from the Internet, it allows the user to create a range of drag-and-drop or multiple-choice tests.

Sound Forge. This software allows you to record and edit sound files with ease.

Word for Windows. Few people make full use of this software. For example, you can attach sound files to bring the text to life or use the "Insert" function to add comment boxes that appear automatically when the cursor moves over a particular word. You can also add hypertext links that automatically take the user to relevant websites at the click of a button or simply use the highlight function to present key vocabulary in different colors.

How Communication Technology Can Support the Accelerated Learning Cycle

Outlined in this section are a few examples of how communication technology can support each part of the four-stage Accelerated Learning Cycle. These are by no means exhaustive but should provide a useful starting point.

Connection Phase

PowerPoint review. Set up a PowerPoint presentation containing key vocabulary and images from the previous lesson or series of lessons. Set the slides to scroll—that is, automatically to fade through black and move on to the next slide every five seconds. Add contextualizing or simply upbeat background music. You now have a highly engaging start to the lesson that reminds students about the learning they have been doing as they come through the classroom door.

Drag-and-drop matching. Students use a mouse to drag and drop labels onto a diagram or to match key vocabulary with definitions. The first student through the door begins, then after dragging and dropping the first label, gets to choose who goes next. This ensures that everyone is on their toes.

Image search. Use the Google image search function to access pictures connected to any topic almost instantaneously. If the connection is tenuous, even better; get students to suggest possible links between the image and what they have been studying.

Online video. Spice up the presentation of new information with an online video; for example, show a two-minute clip of black-and-white footage of Buzz Aldrin on the moon or a recording of Martin Luther King in action.

Activation Phase

This phase is where the student can make particularly good use of communication technology. If you have only one personal computer in the classroom, then arrange a carousel of activity centers around the room and make communication technology one of them. Students could work in groups of four and spend ten minutes at each learning center before moving on. Here are a range of possible communication technology activities:

PowerPoint presentations. Students create their own PowerPoint presentations that they later use to present their ideas to other students. Or they might create a set of annotated PowerPoint slides that other students can use as a learning resource. They could use Sound Forge software and a microphone to add audio buttons for recording their thoughts out loud.

Surfing. Set up (prescreens) a series of websites for students to visit. They use an online graphic organizer to compare and contrast the information they find on each website.

Writing template. Students use an online writing template to help organize their thoughts. For example, an online newspaper front page is already set up with key-word prompts to help students get started.

Camtasia Studio tutorial. Set up a Camtasia Studio tutorial that takes students through a problem-solving exercise (such as math calculations) before they try to solve some similar problems on their own.

Digital photography. Students use a digital camera to provide a visual document of their work in progress. They can use it later to explain their thinking at each stage of their design process.

Modeling clay animation. Students use modeling clay to make simple models of the stages of a physical process (for example, tectonic plates colliding). They label and photograph each stage with a digital camera, then use image editing software such as Paintshop Pro to edit a short animated sequence illustrating the process.

Demonstration Phase

Many of the activities described in the preceding section can also give students the opportunity to demonstrate their new understanding. Here are a few more ideas:

Online testing. Students answer an online test or quiz that you have prepared using software such as Hot Potatoes. You can set up the tests to be self-grading and to give students immediate feedback.

Testing each other. Students prepare an online test for their classmates to complete (again, using Hot Potatoes or similar software). They have to know the answers to be able to do this.

Concept maps. Students use Inspiration or other software to create a concept map that summarizes their understanding of a topic or module. The concept map should mix images and key ideas and clearly show the connections between various aspects of the topic.

Camtasia Studio tutorial. Students use Camtasia Studio to produce an online tutorial for fellow classmates; for example, they might talk their way through a problem they have solved or interpret a piece of text from a play.

Consolidation Phase

Concept mapmaking. Prepare a skeletal concept map on an interactive whiteboard or transparency. Talk through the map with students and add connections as the discussion progresses.

Concept map overview. Produce a concept map giving an overview of the whole topic. Print out copies and have students work in pairs to highlight the areas they have questions about or to add information they feel has been left out.

Digital photograph groups. Take digital photographs of students working in groups. Display these to the class and use them to discuss group process with the students; for example, "How do we know this group is working really well together?" "Can you explain what you were thinking at this point?"

PowerPoint reinforcement. Scroll PowerPoint slides containing key vocabulary, images, and photos of students learning to summarize and reinforce key points from the lesson.

Using Communication Technology as a Staff Planning Tool

Creating an online lesson planning tool for staff allows faculty to plan all lessons online and to update them easily. The lessons are also available for anyone to use, including substitute teachers, and resources for the lesson can be linked to the lesson plan so that they are a mere mouse click away. The sample lesson planning template on the following page shows how one school has interpreted the four-stage Accelerated Learning Cycle to create structure that puts good practice in the right order and makes it explicit.

The completed lesson plan template would be displayed to the whole class via an interactive whiteboard or data projection. Links to Internet and intranet are built in and accessible at a keystroke. Each stage of the cycle can be blanked out if you wish not to show it to the class in advance.

Blank Lesson Planning Template

Lessons last either 55 minutes or 110 minutes.

Relevant music, video clip, key questions, or task loaded in advance for instant access.

Goals can be negotiated with the class if desired. Learning goals are cross-referenced against the appropriate level of Bloom's taxonomy.

An interactive whiteboard is ideal for this section.

There are constant reminders to integrate communication technology in the lesson!

Homework is addressed in the planning process.

Timing	
Connect the Learning ◂	
The Big Picture	

Share the Learning *Goals* *Content* ◂ *Skills*	**By the end of this lesson students will be able to**	**Bloom's Taxonomy** *6. Evaluation* *5. Synthesis* *4. Analysis* *3. Application* *2. Comprehension* *1. Knowledge*

Introduce New Information *VAK* ◂	
Activity *Multiple Intelligences* *Higher-Order Thinking Skills* *Closed/Open* ——— *teacher directed* *student constructed* *Opportunities for communication technology?*	
Demonstrate Your New Understanding *Opportunities for communication technology?*	
Review/Debrief/Preview ▸*Opportunities for communication technology?*	
Assessment for Learning	
Home Learning ▸ *Opportunities for communication technology?*	
Resources	

Accelerated Learning: A User's Guide ©2005 Crown House Publishing Ltd.

Designing Accelerated Learning Web Pages

There are now more pages of information on the World
Wide Web than there are people on the planet.

1. Ask the question, "Is my content suited to an interactive medium?" Many so-called learning websites consist of worksheets, scanned text, and out-of-date links. Is this really what you want?

2. Next, ask, "If I took the content of my website and taught it as a live lesson, would I leave the room proud of what I had achieved?"

3. Do not delude yourself into thinking that because something is on a screen it is somehow better!

4. Always apply the KISS of (learning) life to any online content: Keep it simple, stupid!

5. Use the Accelerated Learning Cycle to help structure your design. This ensures you build in connecting activities; each input is composed of different visual, auditory, and tactile stimuli; there are opportunities to demonstrate understanding; and a consolidation review is built in.

6. Never paste in whole pages of text unmodified. Learning online requires more summaries, more visuals, more reflective questions, and more navigation cues.

7. Locate your pages within navigation windows so that learners can immediately see where they are and how it links to the big picture.

8. Research suggests that a learner can easily manage three windows open at any one time. You can have a main window with your body text; a vertical right-hand side window that carries short summaries, visuals, and links; and a top horizontal window that shows where the learner is on the site.

9. Use an open, easily readable, and modern-looking font that is consistent throughout your website. Avoid changing fonts unnecessarily.

10. Avoid words like *work, test, study, concentration,* and *effort* in your guidance; replace them with vocabulary that is more appropriate to an online experience: *learning, review, access, share, celebrate, scorecard, browse, broker, chat, search, spam, download, upgrade, portal,* and *conference.*

11. Use recurring and recognizable icons to represent summaries, must-know content, key vocabulary, self-test questions, picture galleries, and sample answers.

12. Do not use more than three basic colors on one page.

13. Work on a ratio of one visual to every 250 words. At the very least, break the text every 250 words.

14. Place visuals and highlighted quotations on the right-hand side of the page.

15. Place a one-paragraph summary at the beginning of a chunk of text and place it on the upper right-hand side of the screen.

16. Preview the key learning and key vocabulary at the beginning of the text.

17. Within the text, link key vocabulary to definitions so that one click will bring up the meaning of a word.

18. Alongside each visual place a question. Link the answer such that the learner can access it by clicking on the visual or the question.

19. Have separate picture gallery pages so that visual learners can go through a picture trail and experience the information in a picture sequence.

20. Avoid meaningless activities that do not need a computer—word searches, crosswords or cloze sentences—unless they are interactive and integral to your learning outcomes.

21. Time how long it takes you to read through the text and do the activities yourself. For every eight minutes you take, build in a recommended break for your online learner, who by then will have spent at least 20 minutes staring, head locked at the screen.

22. Make each learning break either integrated in the learning or a rewarding and fun physical activity.

Examples of Accelerated Learning Lesson Plans

No one is stopped in the street by a grateful former student eager to thank you for a memorable worksheet.

The following lessons have been planned using a template based on the four-stage learning cycle.

Topic

Concept maps

Timing

two 55-minute lessons

Materials needed

- Colored pens
- notebook paper
- textbook or class notes
- clothesline and clothespins

CONNECT	
Create the learning environment (display, language, groups, mood, furniture).	Display a concept map you have produced.
Connect (connect learning to previous lesson or to students' prior experience, or stimulate thinking about learning to come; 2- or 3-minute activity at beginning of lesson).	Have students compare concept maps they have done with yours or write down what they think are the most important points to remember when designing a concept map.
Agree on the learning goals/big picture first *(within 5 min. of start of lesson)* • What will students be able to do at the end of the lesson that they could not do at the beginning? • How does this chunk of learning fit into the whole topic/context?	**What I'm Looking For** is for you to practice your concept-mapping skills by creating a unique concept map of the information I will give you. **This Is Because** concept mapping is an important review technique that will help you to make sense of information as you prepare for your exams.

ACTIVATE

Introduction *(VAK, max 10 min.)* Present new information/scene setting/stimulus/ hook through as many senses as possible.	Review what a successful concept map looks like and reinforce some of the important points from the sample map. Then show a different map and use it to emphasize what makes a good concept map and how it can be useful.
Activities *(large part of lesson)* The search for meaning ◎ Use multiple intelligences ◎ Chunk information ◎ Review learning between each activity	Students choose a topic from the subject textbook or class notes and construct a concept map of the information. Students produce a draft map first, then the whole class reviews. Then they produce their final best efforts.

DEMONSTRATE

Show what you know *(large part of lesson)* An opportunity for students to demonstrate their new understanding	Groups of students examine their concept maps, select the best one from the group, and pin it on a clothesline stretched across the front of the classroom. They must be able to justify their group's choice.

CONSOLIDATE

Review Reflect Recall —not just what you learned but how you learned it.	Students share their concept maps with a partner, explaining the connections between items as they trace them with a finger (pole-bridging).

Topic

Salt

Timing

two 55-minute lessons

Materials needed

- Box of sea salt
- pictures of salted items such as bag of salted potato chips, pretzels, canned foods, the ocean
- magnifying glasses
- chalkboard, whiteboard, or chart paper
- Bag of sugar for comparison and melt test

- Crucibles, heatproof mats, goggles, Bunsen burners for melt test
- Straws, clear tape, index stock, and colored pens
- Software (optional): PowerPoint, New Media
- sticky notes
- digital camera

example

CONNECT	
Create the learning environment (display, language, groups, mood, furniture).	Arrange the furniture to accommodate groups of 4 or 5.
Connect (connect learning to previous lesson or to students' prior experience, or stimulate thinking about learning to come; 2- or 3-minute activity at beginning of lesson).	Display pictures that have some (obvious or obscure) connection with salt. (You can create a PowerPoint presentation of scrolling pictures.) Ask groups of students to guess the topic of the lesson based on the picture clues and justify their guesses. Guide them toward the correct answer (if necessary)
Agree on the learning goals/big picture first *(within 5 min. of start of lesson)* - What will students be able to do at the end of the lesson that they could not do at the beginning? - How does this chunk of learning fit into the whole topic/context?	What I'm Looking For is for you to begin to understand the chemistry of salt and the nature of an ionic bond, as well as to see that chemistry can be an interesting and relevant subject that you may want to learn more about. This Is Because salt forms a large part of our diet; it is in nearly everything we eat—chips, canned foods, and so on. Salt is all around us—look at the world's oceans, full of salt! Produce a bag of sea salt. Give each student a little to look at under a magnifying glass, feel, and taste. Ask them to draw a salt crystal. Ask what students might like to find out about salt. Ask why it might be interesting or important to find out something about salt. With the class, develop specific learning goals and criteria for success. Write these on the board or chart paper and display them throughout the lesson.

ACTIVATE

Introduction

(VAK, max 10 min.)

Present new information/scene setting/stimulus/ hook through as many senses as possible.

Activities

(large part of lesson)

The search for meaning

- ◉ Use multiple intelligences
- ◉ Chunk information
- ◉ Review learning between each activity

Experiment: Melt Test

Students compare the physical properties of salt with those of something quite similar (sugar). They discover that although the substances look the same (both white, crystalline solids), there are differences: taste, but more important, a melt test establishes that salt does not melt (high melting point) whereas sugar melts easily. Why? *(10 min.)*

To understand why, students find out what salt is made of at an atomic level and how it is held together. Introduce sodium and chlorine. Be dramatic: Sodium is a soft gray metal I can cut with a knife and that "explodes" on contact with water; chlorine is pale yellow, forming a green and poisonous gas. Follow this with a whole-class presentation using New Media software to explore salt at atomic level and to explain ionic bonds. *(10 min.)*

DEMONSTRATE

Show what you know

(large part of lesson)

An opportunity for students to demonstrate their new understanding

Puppet Show Challenge

Write the following challenge on the board or chart paper: Students have been asked to create a puppet show to explain the chemistry of salt to young children (8-year-olds). They will need to make the puppet show engaging and interesting to hold their attention. The children also need to learn important information about the chemistry of salt. Students will have to use their puppet show to explain some quite complex ideas so that the youngsters can understand them. Lead a discussion to make sure students understand exactly what they need to do, what materials are available, and when they need to have their presentation ready. *(15 min.)*

CONSOLIDATE

Review

Reflect

Recall

—not just what you learned but how you learned it.

Take photos of the puppet shows taking shape. Use these pictures to lead whole-class discussion of some of the fundamental learning from the lesson. Ask students to explain their thinking. *(10 min.)*

Finally, students receive two different colors of sticky notes. On one they write something they found interesting and did not know, and on the other one question they still have.

Topic

Skim 'n Scan

Timing

two 55-minute lessons

Materials needed

- 2 teacher-prepared information sheets on relevant topics, containing combination of graphics, color, and text on 11" x 17" paper
- 11" x 17" paper for each group of 4 students
- colored markers for each group
- for each group, one envelope containing newspaper articles on a specific topic
- teacher-prepared list of questions about the articles

CONNECT	
Create the learning environment (display, language, groups, mood, furniture).	If possible, arrange the furniture to accommodate groups of 4 or 5 and for easy rearrangement into a circle for lesson-closing debriefing.
Connect (connect learning to previous lesson or to students' prior experience, or stimulate thinking about learning to come; 2- or 3-minute activity at beginning of lesson).	Students rearrange the following two sentences so they make sense: - **Skim** rapidly general for impression a main the ideas of look through text - **Scan** rapidly text from by locating out pick words information specific key
Agree on the learning goals/big picture first *(within 5 min. of start of lesson)* - What will students be able to do at the end of the lesson that they could not do at the beginning? - How does this chunk of learning fit into the whole topic/context?	The object of the next two lessons is to introduce **skim** and **scan** reading techniques, which will be useful throughout your school life and when reading exam questions. By the end of the next two lessons, you will be able to confidently use **scan** and **skim** reading techniques on a variety of texts to find useful information quickly.

ACTIVATE	
Introduction *(VAK, max 10 min.)* Present new information/scene setting/stimulus/hook through as many senses as possible.	Information retrieval thinking skills activity: In groups of 4, students number off from 1 to 4. Each group has a blank sheet of 11" x 17" paper and is challenged to replicate the information sheet you have covered at the front of the classroom. Number 1s come to the front and view the information sheet for 30 seconds before it is covered up. They return and share the information with group for 2 min. before number 2s are called up, and so on.

ACTIVATE *(continued from previous page)*

Activities

(large part of lesson)

The search for meaning

- ◎ Use multiple intelligences
- ◎ Chunk information
- ◎ Review learning between each activity

Debrief the process: What strategies did the group employ to access all the information in the given time? What about the way the information was laid out helped them to do this? (For example, key vocabulary underlined or bolded, use of color, pictures, layout, headings, subheadings.) Does this have any implications for the way they prepare or lay out notes as they study for exams? Using what they have learned from this debriefing, students now try to replicate slightly more complicated information. Preview this activity by suggesting they first discuss strategy in their groups.

Repeat the exercise using the second information sheet.

Quickly review the exercise: Was it more difficult? If so, why? Did they look for key information (scanning)? Or did they just try to get a general overview very quickly (skimming)? Or did they do a combination of both?

DEMONSTRATE

Show what you know

(large part of lesson)

An opportunity for students to demonstrate their new understanding

In this exercise students try to use both techniques. Give each group of 4 an envelope containing newspaper articles on a specific topic and a list of questions to answer about it.

1. Students skim the information to get a general overview.
2. They answer as many questions as possible.
3. They identify what they still need to know.
4. They scan the articles for the specific information needed.
5. They fill in the missing information on the worksheet.
6. The group agrees on the most pertinent information and writes a short newspaper article about the topic.

CONSOLIDATE

Review

Reflect

Recall

—not just what you learned but how you learned it.

Debrief the lesson in a circle. Where might students use the skills they have learned? Can they give specific examples of where these skills have or would have been useful in other curriculum areas? How might they change their test-preparation strategies in light of this experience? Ask students to practice the skills of scanning and skimming as many times as possible over the next 2 weeks in other subject areas.

Your Questions Answered

Be expedient in strategy and consistent in principles.

Q: Wasn't all this around in the 1960s and 1970s?

A: Certainly we have been talking about different concepts such as active learning, flexible learning environments, and taking into account individual needs for many years, but the Accelerated Learning framework has taken things much further. First, it is based on scientific theories about learning, including understanding of how the brain functions (for example, high challenge but low threat), as well as what motivates learners. Second, it puts disparate ideas into a very effective sequence of activities (the stages in the cycle) that bring a coherence, pace, and rigor to lesson preparation. With the cycle as a framework or planning vehicle, we put good practice into the right order.

Q: Isn't all this a restriction on the way teachers teach?

A: Well, one would hope that all teachers plan and structure their lessons. One would also hope that this planning and structure would be based on something tangible, like how effective learning happens! If so, the framework provides a particularly useful support structure. But, of course, that is only the start. Teachers have absolute freedom to draw on their full repertoire of teaching strategies in order to make effective learning happen. Nobody is telling teachers that they must use techniques such as Mind Mapping, role-play, collaborative learning, and so on. Those decisions are left to their professional judgment. Asking which teaching technique is best is analogous to asking which tool is best—a hammer, a screwdriver, a knife, or pliers. In teaching, as in carpentry, the selection of tools depends on the task at hand and the materials one is working with. It follows that the more tools you have in your toolbox, and the more you understand and appreciate their use, the more likely you are to get the job done. And some classes on some days, as well as some individuals, require a very specialized wrench!

Q: Does this mean that whole-class "traditional" teaching is wrong?

A: By no means. Book work and lectures can be wonderfully efficient modes of transmitting new information, exciting the imagination, and honing critical thinking. But lectures work less well with visual learners than with auditory learners, so I would hope that anyone giving a lecture applies the seeing, hearing, and doing principle and has plenty of visual aids and perhaps offers the opportunity for moving around, rearranging or reordering sticky notes, and so on! Also, lectures will not help students to demonstrate their understanding—an important stage of the cycle. And learners need time to reflect not just on what they have learned, but also on how they have learned it!

Q: But surely there is a best way to teach, isn't there?

A: We have long known that variety is the spice of learning, but now we have a theory showing us why and how different activities appeal to different learners and can be used for different purposes. The point is not variety for the sake of variety but specific activities targeted to a purpose. The beauty of the cycle is that it focuses us on how people learn and moves us beyond "either/or" teaching methods, such as individual versus group-based, lecture-based versus inquiry-based. There is no universal best teaching practice. We need to select from a variety, a repertoire, of teaching strategies with a particular purpose in mind. For example, we know that humans are social animals and that most natural learning does not just happen on its own but through working with someone else (for example, apprenticeship) or learning from a larger group, as children do in a family. It would be important, therefore, to build this understanding into our range of teaching strategies. In fact, that is how the interpersonal learner learns best. We may select a variety of teaching strategies to appeal to all different types of learners within the same lesson, say through a carousel of activities in the Activation stage of the cycle, or perhaps we do only one particular type of activity appealing to, say, the visual learner, but next time we see the group we do a mainly kinesthetic activity. The key idea here is that teaching is planned and sequential, a conscious choice of activity with a purpose in mind based on a knowledge of the different learning styles in our classroom.

Q: How long should a cycle take?

A: Ideally, within a single lesson (fifty-five or sixty minutes, minimum) you would go through all the stages in the cycle; however, some teachers prefer to use a double lesson per cycle. In some cases you would go through the cycle over a longer period but all the while you would remind the students of the stages they have gone through and the stages to come.

Q: We have a particular problem in this school with boys' achievement. Will this approach help?

A: Here is a list of some "boy friendly" practices:

- Devise clearly structured lessons, connected to their learning with clear goals.
- Evaluate the gender bias of resources and topics of study.
- Enhance self-esteem through rewards and displays of work.
- Allow movement with a purpose; tell the class why movement will help them to learn.
- Provide opportunities to learn by "trying out" rather than being told about—that is, investigative learning.
- Build on boys' spatial awareness: Give them success with plans and maps; teach them to use Mind Maps.

- Build up a collection of objects for students to touch.
- Act out stories, events, and concepts.
- Allow for competition.
- Use communication technology as part of teaching and learning.
- Put the learning in context: Why are we learning this? Show the big picture.
- Break the learning into chunks.
- Develop peer tutoring systems, including paired writing.
- Introduce shared reading: pair competent male readers with those who have low self-esteem.
- Monitor teacher talk. There is evidence to suggest that, although teachers believe they treat boys and girls the same, they rarely do.
- Make references to appropriate role models. Steven Biddulph, an Australian behavioral psychologist specializing in bringing up boys, says that children are "role-seeking missiles" (see, for example, Biddulph 1998).
- Have high expectations. Build in challenge to engage and enhance performance and set sequential, achievable targets.
- Talk to the boys themselves to discover their expectations and aspirations, their fears and concerns, and support and encourage them every step of the way.

Notice how well these practices relate to Accelerated Learning techniques!

Q: **How do I find time to prepare these lessons?**

A: You prepare lessons anyway, right? Like all teachers, you want your students to enjoy their lessons, be involved, and make progress. The Accelerated Learning Cycle provides a framework to achieve this outcome successfully. At first, lesson planning will take time, but as you use the framework and the tips in this book, you will find it becomes second nature. A good analogy is learning how to drive. At first, it took time and conscious effort, but now it is almost automatic.

You may also wish to try reducing grading and spending the saved time on preparation. See "Smart Grading" on pages 54–59 for ideas. Get others involved so that you can swap ideas and lessons. Take it slowly at first. Try one lesson per week and work up to one per day. Take it at your own pace. Enjoy seeing your creativity come to life!

Q: **Does it work with all students, even the alienated ones?**

A: There is always a temptation to give difficult students "busy work"—copying, making notes, drawing diagrams—to keep them occupied. This work has nothing to do with learning and everything to do with control, and in the long run will lead to more alienation because the learners are not engaged with the work. Good Accelerated Learning is motivating for students and will make alienation less of an issue.

Well-focused teaching goes a long way toward meeting the needs of students of all abilities, including the gifted and talented and those with special educational needs. Accelerated Learning is really for all and is often most appreciated by alienated students because it pays close attention to individual learners—their preconceptions, learning styles, self-esteem, and progress. As such, it better meets the needs of those learners most alienated by so-called traditional methods that concentrate on the needs of the class rather than of the individual. It acknowledges particularly the needs of the kinesthetic learner, those who like to learn by doing.

Introducing Accelerated Learning into Your School

We see, we feel, we change.

In introducing any significant change—and changing the way people teach is pretty significant—there are a number of golden rules:

- All change is emotionally charged. You are asking people to make a leap of faith. They need to see, feel, and experience the change in order to accept and make sense of it.

- Change needs to be top down and bottom up. Principals and department heads have power and access to resources. They need to be worked with and on. Ignore them at your peril. People will resist top-down-only change. Some of the "Indians," as well as the "chiefs," need to be involved and enthusiastic!

- Think big but start small—in a grade level or department, for example. Then use success to breed success and bring more on board.

- It is not how you see the situation that's important, what's important is how others see it. Constantly check that they understand what is needed. Address their anxieties and provide resources, training, and above all, time for preparation and reflection.

- Change occurs through different stages, described in the remainder of this section. All are important and need careful consideration. All have traps best avoided!

Stage 1: Getting Others to See the Need for Change

People are less likely to change what they do in response to analysis that shifts their thinking than to a truth that influences their feelings. In other words, willingness to change is an emotional response, which should not come as a surprise to an Accelerated Learning teacher. Educators will tend to think that their present methods have worked for them in the past, so there is no need to change. How do we help colleagues to see a different and better future?

The classic mistake is to present too complex a picture—almost a "laundry list" of why change is needed. In this case what often happens is that people zero in on the not so important contrasts rather than the critical ones. The way around this is to adopt the KISS principle, which stands for "Keep it simple, stupid"!

Focus on what you think are the core contrasts between present practices and what Accelerated Learning will do in the future. Do not dilute them with too much complexity! For example, key advantages might be

- students will be more involved and engaged in their learning.
- you will know whether students really understand what they have learned.
- Accelerated Learning caters to the different learning styles of our students.
- the cycle puts good practice in the right order.

Make sure that the experience involves as many of the senses as possible. In particular, seeing the change in action makes for a memorable experience. Thus, these strategies would be effective:

- videos of Accelerated Learning in action, showing student responses
- visiting a school that is using Accelerated Learning techniques. There is nothing like seeing a real school with real students in action and talking to the staff and students about the experience.
- surveying the students for their present views on their learning experience. How would they like it improved?

You cannot bulldoze change. Successfully implementing educational change needs both top-down and bottom-up strategies. According to Professor Michael Fullan, an international authority on change, top-down strategies alone bring grief but no relief and bottom-up strategies alone bring the odd spurt that eventually becomes inert (Fullan 1993).

In trying to persuade people of the need to introduce Accelerated Learning, remember the iceberg principle and show only the tip of the argument, keeping the rest in reserve. Perhaps present no more than three or four key points but remember that saying them once will not be enough. The key points may well have to be revisited half a dozen times before colleagues really come to accept them.

Remember, too, the need to bring on board key players who wield power and influence (principals, heads of department). It is very difficult to work around them, so involve them in identifying the problem and help them to come to your solution!

Two tools useful for starting the debate on the need for change are the sigmoid curve and a simple compare-and-contrast matrix of natural learning versus secondary school learning. These are effective because both are visual and both can be related to people on a personal (emotional) level. The sigmoid curve, for example, can also be used to chart the rise and (eventual) fall of the local football team (Do you bring in young players when the team is doing well or when things are in decline?) and the problems of struggling corporations. Moving jobs when you are happy and successful seems to be good advice when contrasted with the desperation workers often feel when "trying to get out." The important point here is that it is often best to change when things are going well, because if you do not change, the odds are things will get worse and then change will be very much harder. This is a useful argument to use with good or complacent departments or schools.

The Sigmoid Curve

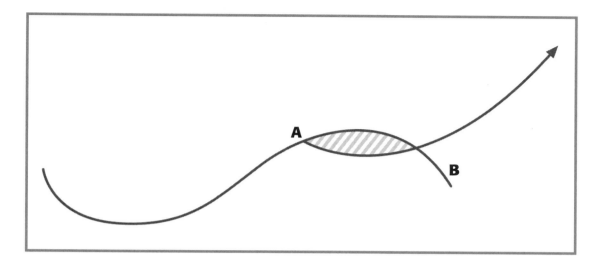

Handy (1994) suggests that most organizations rise and fall or expand and contract in a way very similar to a sine wave. The challenge for leadership in successful schools is to spot when the organization is at point A and to engineer the situation so that the school does not rest on its laurels when it is improving. It must take the risk of moving on to a new sigmoid curve, rather than waiting to change until it is moving downward at point B. Handy expresses this as follows:

> The right place to start that second curve is at point A, where there is time, as well as the resources and the energy, to get the curve through its initial explorations and floundering before the first curve begins to dip downwards. That would seem obvious; were it not for the fact that at point A all the messages coming through to the individual or the institution are that everything is going fine, that it would be folly to change when the current recipes are working so well. All that we know of change, be it personal change or change in organizations, tells us that the real energy for change only comes when you are looking disaster in the face, at point B on the first curve. At this point, however, it is going to require a mighty effort to drag oneself up to where, by now, one should be on the second curve. (Handy 1994, 5 1–52)

Natural Learning versus Secondary School Learning

Also resonant with the personal experiences of parents, teachers, or children is the natural learning versus secondary school learning chart. If, as seems reasonable, we are all hardwired to learn, then little of "natural learning" survives the transfer to secondary-level education, as shown in the following chart. Accelerated Learning can help to correct this balance!

Natural Learning	Secondary-Level Learning
concrete experiences, images	abstract concepts
holographic processing	verbal processing
learning by doing and imitation	linear processing
learning in context	learning by reading
learning with others	learning out of context
	learning by yourself

Stage 2: Seeing the Need to Change but Failing to Move

As people move nearer to making a significant change, they tend to get more anxious about it. If we fail to address people's natural anxieties and concerns, we will get what is known as the implementation dip, where things do not start at all well. Most of us do not like the thought of doing something new poorly, especially if we are already good at what we're currently doing. We should not underestimate what is often initially well concealed—the fear of looking stupid or incompetent.

An old joke goes something like this: On a dark night a man has lost his ring and a passerby sees him searching and pauses to ask, "What did you lose?" "My ring" comes the reply. The conversation continues: "Where did you lose it?" "Way over there" the desperate searcher answers. "Then why are you looking here?" queries the passerby. "Because this is where the light is" replies the hopeless searcher. In schools, we often stay where the light is, even when we recognize that it is the wrong place. Similarly, we often stick to what we are good at even when we see it has become irrelevant.

So what do you do?

1. Address directly anxieties and concerns. Listen carefully to what people have to say. They may see something that you in your zeal have overlooked.
2. Remove any obstacles:
   Lack of time. Provide time for teachers to plan and review together by rearranging the school week to finish early on one day. Divide meetings into operational and strategic segments. The urgent often drives out the important, so safeguard your strategic time for planning and review.
   Lack of expertise. Appoint learning coaches who work with teachers in the classrooms. Two in the classroom can help overcome discipline fears. Provide professional development and visit other schools.
   Feeling overwhelmed. Think big but start small, giving colleagues time to get used to the innovation. Choose a grade, department, or class to start implementing Accelerated Learning. Then build on the success.
3. A classic mistake is that since you see the need for change, you assume that everyone else does too. It is at this stage that you need to check for understanding. How clearly do your colleagues see where they are going?

Ask them to describe each key element of the Accelerated Learning Cycle. Then ask them what implementing it will require from them in terms of personal abilities. One school used a scenario challenge (see box) to check whether the faculty had a clear understanding of Accelerated Learning. This is often a good and safe way to address concerns and anxieties.

Scenario Challenge

Essential Question

In what way does Accelerated Learning provide a framework for effective teaching and learning?

Challenge

You must present the case for Accelerated Learning to an audience of teachers, organized into groups of four or five, at a school where you have just been hired. The aim of your presentation will be to convince them that they should adopt this framework as a means of developing teaching and learning in their school. This is the first time your audience has heard of the model. Although the teachers are not cynical, they may well be critical and ask such questions as

- Won't students get sick of the same kind of lessons all the time?
- How can I sustain this kind of teaching?
- How does this model encourage collaborative learning?
- Will I be able to cover the curriculum content in time?
- Is Accelerated Learning suitable for the most able and least able students?

Presentation Criteria

Your presentation should last for a maximum of ten minutes and include

- an explanation of the principles underpinning Accelerated Learning.
- practical examples of classroom practice.
- an attempt to answer the preceding questions.
- a graphic or visual image or diagram that your entire audience can view and that each group can talk about.
- a memorable quotation, saying, or slogan that "hooks" your audience and forms part of your graphic or visual image.
- a simple paragraph containing no more than three sentences summarizing why you think this approach can make learning much more interesting and effective.

Note: All members of each group should take part in the presentation. Finally, have fun and remember that the most memorable presentations are humorous in some way.

Stage 3: Starting to Lose Momentum

People get tired! Change requires energy and effort. There is a danger that things can drift and momentum falter. At this stage there is a need for

champions: colleagues close to the action who provide encouragement and support. Perhaps they might team-teach in colleagues' classrooms as learning coaches, using techniques such as "you plan and I'll teach to your plan" and then reversing it: "I'll plan and you teach."

celebrations: sharing successes and making much of the students' reactions. One strategy might be to make a video of a successful lesson or an interview with the students where they identify what has changed and what they like about the new approach. The more the outcomes of change are visible, measurable, and unambiguous the better.

rewards: acknowledgment of colleagues' efforts; for example, allocate them a laptop, or share successful lesson plans, thereby saving individual planning time. Cramlington Community High School rewards staff who are observed teaching using Accelerated Learning with a $150 credit that they can use for professional development or teaching materials. Faculty can accumulate their credits, and when they wish to cash them in, the school matches the cost of the training or purchase dollar for dollar. This enables faculty to finance professional development opportunities they otherwise could not afford or to purchase for exclusive school use items such as digital cameras or VCRs.

Stage 4: Embedding the Change so It Becomes Part of the Whole Culture

Change is a journey not a blueprint.
—Michael Fullan

It is important to pay particular attention to hiring and orientation of new faculty. By being clear about what you are looking for, you are more likely to get a match whereby new faculty joining the school are in tune with the culture of Accelerated Learning. The hiring process could involve interviewees planning a lesson using the Accelerated Learning Cycle, and the orientation process might consist of a full day's training. New initiatives within the school need to be aligned to Accelerated Learning. If the principal periodically observes classes when doing performance reviews, the lesson observation form used for this purpose can be designed to keep good teaching and learning at the forefront of everyone's thoughts. Similarly, communication technology should support Accelerated Learning. Here is a valuable peg on which to hang the communication technology hat!

The school or departmental development plan should also be firmly rooted in priorities for successful teaching and learning. Accelerated Learning should be at the heart of the school or department, and this focus needs to be reflected in the documentation that the school or department produces. And, of course, really clever administrators can model the cycle in departmental and staff meetings and on in-service days. Other ways to keep Accelerated Learning at the forefront of all colleagues' minds can include

- buying staff planning books where the introductory pages are customized and include handy hints on Accelerated Learning.
- publishing a school "Teaching for Learning" newsletter. If it is useful, practical, stimulating, and readable, such a newsletter can keep teaching and learning visible and salient.
- inviting colleagues from other schools to observe lessons. There is nothing like the approval of peers to build confidence and make teachers feel they are really doing something worthwhile. Being observed also keeps them on their toes!

It is important to ensure that what you think is going on is actually going on! Formal monitoring of classrooms is one way to do this, as is an informal "walk through," stopping to talk to teachers and looking at students' work and the learning in which they are engaged. Finally, regular surveys of the students' views through questionnaires provide invaluable data. Publish the results.

The classic mistake at this stage is to think you have the change licked and move on to something else. Preaching to the converted, far from being a superfluous activity, is vital. Preachers do it every Sunday! The strengthening of the commitment and morale of those on board is essential in order both to bind them more closely and to make them more effective proponents of Accelerated Learning. You never quite know you have arrived at your destination until people start saying, "Accelerated Learning? Well, that's just the way we do things around here."

Appendix —————————————————

Resources

In the Appendix You Will Find

▶ Recommended Reading

▶ Useful Websites

▶ Teacher Questionnaire

▶ Lesson Planning Forms

Recommended Reading

A Selection of Books by the Authors

Smith, A. 2001. *The ALPS Approach Resource Book.* Stafford, U.K.: Network Educational Press.

————. 2002. *Accelerated Learning in Practice.* San Clemente, Calif.: Kagan Publishing.

————. 2005. *The Brain's Behind It.* Norwalk, Conn.: Crown House Publishing.

Smith, A., and N. Call. 1999. *The ALPS Approach: Accelerated Learning in Primary Schools.* Stafford, U.K.: Network Educational Press.

Smith, A., and B. Lucas. 2002. *Help Your Child to Succeed.* Stafford, U.K.: Network Educational Press

Smith, A., and P. Lyseight-Jones. 2003. *Moving On: A Quality Framework for Accelerated Learning.* Bourne End, U.K.: Alite Ltd.

Wise, D., and M. Lovatt. 2001. *Creating an Accelerated Learning School.* Stafford, U.K.: Network Educational Press.

20 Must-Have Books for Your School Library

Bransford, J., A. Brown, and R. Cocking. 1999. *How People Learn: Brain, Mind, Experience and School.* Washington, D.C.: U.S. National Research Council.
300-plus pages of quality insights

Call, N., and S. Featherstone. 2002. *The Thinking Child.* Stafford, U.K.: Network Educational Press.
An exposition of brain-based learning for early learners

Carter, R. 1999. *Mapping the Mind.* Berkeley: University of California Press.
An excellent summary to date for the lay reader

Caviglioli, O., and I. Harris. 2003. *Thinking Visually.* Markham, Canada: Pembroke Publishers.
A resource that moves beyond Mind Mapping; looks terrific

Claxton, G. 2003. *Building Learner Power.* Bristol, U.K.: TLO Ltd.
The author's case for a more holistic view of lifelong learning

Costa, A., ed. 2001. *Developing Minds: A Resource Book for Teaching Thinking.* Alexandria, Va.: ASCD.
A collection of articles for those who teach thinking

Gilbert, I. 2002. *Essential Motivation.* London: Routledge.
Easily accessible thoughts about motivation in the classroom

Ginnis, P. 2005. *The Teacher's Toolkit.* Norwalk, Conn.: Crown House Publishing.
A carefully written and thoroughly researched work linking theory to practice

Goleman, D.1995. *Emotional Intelligence: Why It Matters More Than IQ.* New York: Bantam Books.
The book that launched the movement

Goleman, D., P. Boyatzis, and A. McKee. 2002. *Primal Leadership.* Cambridge, Mass.: Harvard Business School Press.
A gift to give your principal

Gopnik, A., A. Meltzoff, and P. Kuhl. 1999. *The Scientist in the Crib: Minds, Brains, and How Children Learn.* New York: William Morrow & Co.
A work that blows a small hole in Piaget's boat!

Greany, T., and J. Rodd. 2003. *Creating a Learning to Learn School.* Stafford, U.K.: Network Educational Press.
Useful resource that emerged from the Learning to Learn project

Howard, P. J. 2000. *The Owner's Manual for the Brain.* 2nd ed. Austin, Tex.: Bard Press.
Comprehensive and very readable overview of the psychology and physiology of learning

Mahoney, T. 2003. *Words Work: How to Change Your Language to Improve Behaviour in the Classroom.* Bancyfelin, Wales: Crown House Publishing.
The use of NLP in schools

Novak, J. 2002. *Inviting Educational Leadership.* Harlow, U.K.: Pearson Education.
And why not invite your administrators to read it?

Perkins, D. 1992. *Smart Schools.* New York: Free Press.
A Harvard professor's view on thinking schools

Rockett, M., and S. Percival. 2002. *Thinking for Learning.* Stafford, U.K.: Network Educational Press.
Good overview of different practical approaches to teaching thinking skills

Rupp, R. 1998. *Committed to Memory.* New York: Crown.
Concise overview of memory techniques

Senge, P. 2000. *Schools That Learn.* New York: Doubleday.
Fifth discipline field book for educators

Vos, J., and G. Dryden. 2001. *The Learning Revolution.* Stafford, U.K.: Network Educational Press.
An overview of some world trends in learning

Useful Websites

Learning Environments

www.bottledwater.org   *International Bottled Water Association*
www.sleepresearchsociety.org   *Sleep Research Society*
www.braingym.org   *Dennison's Brain Gym® organization*

Learning Styles

www.gregorc.com   *Anthony Gregorc*
www.mind-map.com   *Tony Buzan*
www.thomasarmstrong.com   *Thomas Armstrong*
www.advisorteam.com/user/ktsintro.asp   *Kiersey Temperament Sorter*
www.knowyourtype.com   *Myers-Briggs Type Indicator*

Learning for the Future

www.itaa.org   *Information Technology Association of America*

www.pzweb.harvard.edu/Research/Research   *The official Harvard Project Zero site*
www.nestafuturelab.org   *New modes of learning*

Parent Resources

www.allianceforchildhood.net   *Alliance for Childhood*
www.cdipage.com   *The Child Development Institute*

Organizations

www.ialearn.org   *International Alliance for Learning*
www.campaign-for-learning.org.uk   *Campaign for Learning*
www.21learn.org   *21st Century Learning Initiative*
www.ufa.org.uk   *University of the First Age*
www.ascd.org   *Association for Supervision and Curriculum Development*

www.clcrc.com   *The Co-operative Learning Center*

Thinking Skills Approaches

www.modellearning.com   *Mapping techniques*
www.case-network.org   *Cognitive acceleration*
www.thethinkingclassroom.co.uk   *Thinking classrooms in practice*
www.psych.qub.ac.uk/staff/mcguinness.html   *Carol McGuinness and her work*
www.teachingthinking.net   *Robert Fisher's website*
www.edwdebono.com   *Edward de Bono site*
www.simnet.is/heimspekiskolinn/icpic.html   *International Council of Philosophical Inquiry with Children*

Learning and Motivation

www.eiconsortium.org/members/goleman.htm   *Emotional intelligence*
www.learningfirst.org   *Learning First Alliance*
www.casel.org   *Social and emotional learning*
www.stanford.edu/group/CRE/motivation.htm   *Motivation research*

Learning Differences

www.ldresources.com   *Learning disabilities resources*
www.ldonline.org   *Overview of learning disabilities*
www.interdys.org   *International Dyslexia Association*
www.nagc.org   *National Association for Gifted Children*
www.edwebproject.org/edref.mi.intro.html   *Multiple intelligences site*

Learning and Brain Research

www.brainresearch.com   *Recommended for comprehensive links*
www.brainconnection.com   *BrainConnection site*
www.newhorizons.org   *A source for latest thinking on education*
www.jlcbrain.com   *Eric Jensen's website*
www.cainelearning.com   *Geoffrey and Renate Caine's website*
www.apa.org   *American Psychological Association*
www.med.harvard.edu/AANLIB   *The Whole Brain Atlas*
www.science.ca/scientists/Kimura/kimura.html   *Gender and brain organization*
www.cnlmuci.edu   *University of California at Irvine, Center for the Neurobiology of Learning and Memory*

Music and Learning

www.mozartcenter.com/index.html   *Tomatis method*
www.musica.uci.edu   *MuSICA Music and Science Information Computer Archive*

www.mindinst.org/   *MIND Institute Research into the Mozart Effect and Education*

Teacher Questionnaire

Use this questionnaire to reflect on your own practice.

	Usually	Sometimes	Needs Attention
I apply recent research about learning to plan effective lessons.			
I rearrange the furniture in my classroom to facilitate the learning activity.			
My classroom has attractive displays that include students' work.			
I use my classroom displays as a teaching aid.			
I make my students feel welcome when they arrive in the classroom.			
I warn my students when I am going to ask them questions.			
I don't allow my students to put each other down.			
I don't use put-downs or sarcasm in my classroom.			
I establish clear learning goals and display them prominently in my classroom			
I refer to the learning goals throughout the lesson and especially as part of the review.			
I connect the lesson to what has gone before.			
I provide clear signposts for the learning journey (the big picture).			
I make it clear to my students why they should buy in to learning what I am teaching.			
When I present lessons or information, I use visual stimuli.			
I give my students the opportunity to exchange their views and opinions.			
I don't answer my own questions!			
I allow my students time to think when I ask a question.			
I give my students an opportunity for physical movement in my lessons.			
I use feedback throughout my lessons.			
I plan my lessons keeping in mind that students learn in different ways.			

Accelerated Learning: A User's Guide ©2005 Crown House Publishing Company LLC

Teacher Questionnaire *(continued)*

	Usually	Sometimes	Needs Attention
I use collaborative (cooperative) learning techniques.			
I allow time for students to work independently.			
I have whole-class discussions.			
I try to engage my students' emotions through use of evocative music, film, prose, or poetry.			
I use games or activities that involve my students in the lesson.			
I use color in a purposeful way in my lessons.			
I ensure my students have the opportunity to demonstrate their new understanding.			
I review the key learning points in my lessons.			
I try and tease out with my students how they have learned.			

Lesson Planning Forms

This section provides practical resources for teachers. Feel free to photocopy these forms, enlarging them if needed. Use them to plan lessons in the Accelerated Learning Cycle or adapt and change as you see fit.

Topic: _____ Lesson: _____ Date: _____

CONNECT

ACTIVATE

DEMONSTRATE

CONSOLIDATE

Accelerated Learning: A User's Guide ©2005 Crown House Publishing Company LLC

Subject _____ Date _____

	Monday	Tuesday	Wednesday	Thursday	Friday	Resources
CONNECT — **Use input/activity to agree on the following:** 1. What we already know and what would be useful to know (content) 2. How we will learn (process) 3. How today's learning fits into the overall topic (benefits)						
ACTIVATE — **Pose problems and present new information through different channels.** Visual Auditory Kinesthetic Other						
DEMONSTRATE — **Structure activities around the problems posed.** Activity Feedback and review Activity Feedback and review						Assessment
CONSOLIDATE — **Agree on** What has been learned How it has been learned How the learning is useful						

Topic _____ Lesson _____ Date _____

	Resources	
CONNECT **Use input/activity to agree on the following:** 1. What we already know and what would be useful to know (content) 2. How we will learn (process) 3. How today's learning fits into the overall topic (benefits)		
ACTIVATE **Pose problems and present new information through different channels.** Visual Auditory Kinesthetic Other		
DEMONSTRATE **Structure activities around the problems posed.** Activity Feedback and review Activity Feedback and review	Assessment	
CONSOLIDATE **Agree on** What has been learned How it has been learned How the learning is useful		

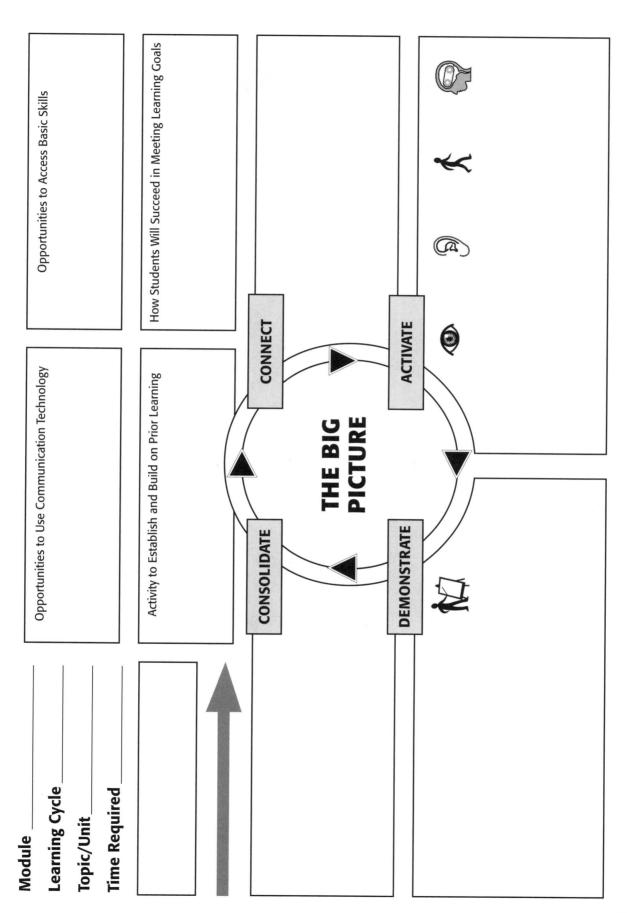

Module _____

Learning Cycle _____

Topic/Unit _____

Time Required _____

Opportunities to Access Basic Skills

How Students Will Succeed in Meeting Learning Goals

Opportunities to Use Communication Technology

Activity to Establish and Build on Prior Learning

THE BIG PICTURE

CONNECT

ACTIVATE

CONSOLIDATE

DEMONSTRATE

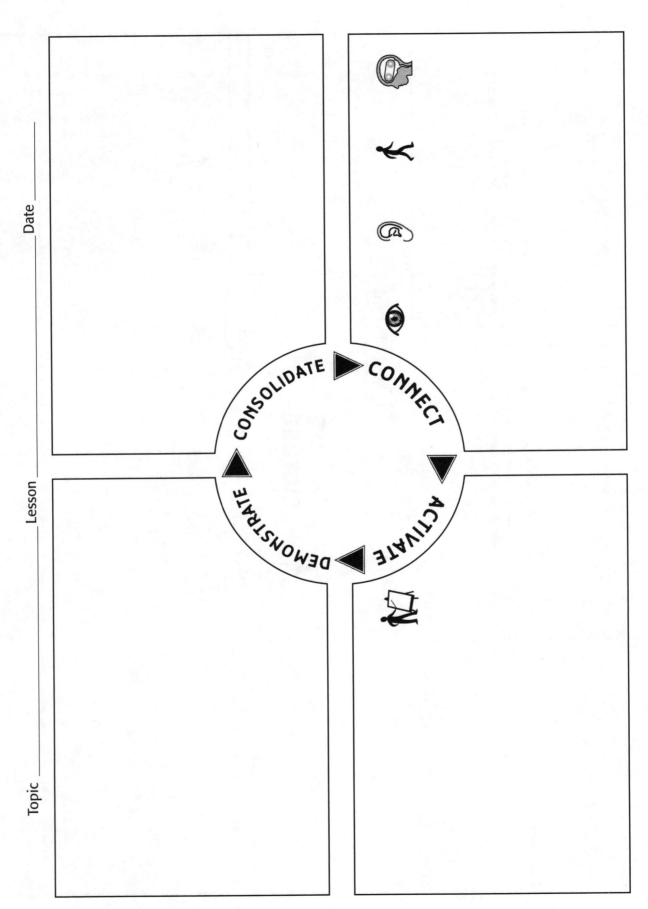

Lesson _____ Date _____

CONNECT		Resources
ACTIVATE		
DEMONSTRATE		Assessment
CONSOLIDATE		

References

Amis, K. 1980. *Jake's Thing.* New York: Penguin.

Assessment Reform Group. 1999. *Assessment for Learning: Beyond the Black Box.* London: Kings College.

Bandler, R. 1992. *Magic in Action.* Capitola, Calif.: Meta Publications.

Biddulph, S. 1998. *Raising Boys: Why Boys Are Different—and How to Help Them Become Happy and Well-Balanced Men.* Berkeley, Calif.: Celestial Arts.

Black, P., and D. Wiliam. 1998. *Inside the Black Box: Raising Standards through Classroom Assessment. Phi Delta Kappan,* October. Available online: www.pdkintl.org/kappan/kbla9810.htm.

Bloom, B. 1956. *The Taxonomy of Educational Objectives.* London: Longman.

Clarke, S. 2001. *Unlocking Formative Assessment.* London: Hodder & Stoughton Educational.

Dunn, R., and K. Dunn. 1978. *Teaching Students through Their Individual Learning Styles.* Englewood Cliffs, N.J.: Prentice-Hall.

Fullan, M. 1993. *Change Forces: Probing the Depth of Educational Reform.* London and New York: Falmer Press.

Gardner, H. 1993. *Multiple Intelligences: The Theory in Practice.* New York: Basic Books.

Ginnis, P. 2005. *The Teacher's Toolkit.* Norwalk, Conn.: Crown House Publishing.

Goleman, D. 1995. *Emotional Intelligence: Why It Matters More Than IQ.* New York: Bantam Books.

Grinder, M. 1991. *Righting the Educational Conveyor Belt.* Portland, Oreg.: Metamorphous Press.

Hattie, J. A. 1992. Measuring the Effects of Schooling. *Australian Journal of Education* 36(1): 5–13.

Hermann, N. 1997. *The Hermann Brain Dominance Instrument.* Lake Lure, N.C.: Hermann International.

Hughes, M. 1999. *Closing the Learning Gap.* Stafford, U.K.: Network Educational Press.

Hyerle, D. 2000. *A Field Guide to Using Visual Tools.* Alexandria, Va.: ASCD.

Kolb, D. 1984. *Experiential Learning: Experience as the Source of Learning Development.* Englewood Cliffs, N.J.: Prentice-Hall.

Lozanov, G. 1978. *Suggestology and Outlines of Suggestopedy.* New York: Gordon & Breach.

————. 1981. *Suggestology and Suggestopedy: Theory and Practice.* Paris: UNESCO.

Marzano, R. 2001. *What Works in Schools.* Alexandria, Va.: ASCD.

McCarthy, B. 1982. *The 4MAT System.* Arlington, Va.: Excel Publishing.

Rose, C., and M. J. Nicholl. 1997. *Accelerated Learning for the 21st Century: The Six-Step Plan to Unlock Your Master-Mind.* New York: Delacorte Press.

Sapolsky, Robert M. 1998. *Why Zebras Don't Get Ulcers: An Updated Guide to Stress, Related Diseases, and Coping.* New York: Freeman.

Vygotsky, L. S. 1978. *Mind in Society.* Cambridge, Mass.: Harvard University Press.

Wenger, W., and R. Poe. 1996. *The Einstein Factor: A Proven New Method for Increasing Your Intelligence.* Rocklin, Calif.: Prima Publications.

Index

About the Authors

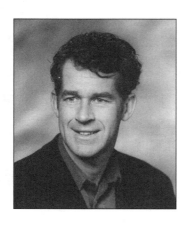

Alistair Smith

is a well-respected and experienced presenter, trainer, and author. He is the chairperson of Alite Ltd., a company he founded to work in the field of motivation, teaching, and learning.

Derek Wise

is headteacher at Cramlington Community High School in Northumberland, England. The school has received special recognition as a 'leading edge school.' He co-authored *Creating an Accelerated Learning School* with Mark Lovatt and is often called upon to present at conferences on leadership and learning.

Mark Lovatt

is deputy headteacher at Cramlington Community High School in Northumberland, England. He has responsibility for teaching and learning, and co-authored *Creating an Accelerated Learning School* with Derek Wise. He frequently participates in education conferences at local and national levels.

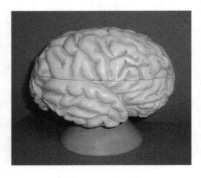
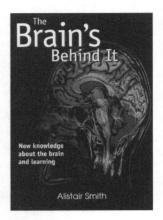